BFI Film Classics

The BFI Film Classics series introduces, interprets and celebrates landmarks of world cinema. Each volume offers an argument for the film's 'classic' status, together with discussion of its production and reception history, its place within a genre or national cinema, an account of its technical and aesthetic importance, and in many cases, the author's personal response to the film.

For a full list of titles in the series, please visit https://www.bloomsbury.com/uk/series/bfi-film-classics/

T0347697

A Taste of Honey

Melanie Williams

THE BRITISH FILM INSTITUTE
Bloomsbury Publishing Plc
50 Bedford Square, London, WC1B 3DP, UK
1385 Broadway, New York, NY 10018, USA
29 Earlsfort Terrace, Dublin 2, Ireland

BLOOMSBURY is a trademark of Bloomsbury Publishing Plc

First published in Great Britain 2023 by Bloomsbury on behalf of the
British Film Institute
21 Stephen Street, London W1T 1LN
www.bfi.org.uk

The BFI is the lead organisation for film in the UK and the distributor of Lottery funds for film.
Our mission is to ensure that film is central to our cultural life, in particular by supporting and
nurturing the next generation of filmmakers and audiences. We serve a public role which covers
the cultural, creative and economic aspects of film in the UK.

Cover artwork: © Rania Moudarres
Series cover design: Louise Dugdale
Series text design: Ketchup/SE14
Images from *A Taste of Honey* (Tony Richardson, 1961), Woodfall Film Productions. Film stills by
Raymond Hearne courtesy BFI National Archive

A catalogue record for this book is available from the British Library.

A catalog record for this book is available from the Library of Congress.

ISBN: PB: 978-1-8390-2155-8
        ePDF: 978-1-8390-2158-9
        ePUB: 978-1-8390-2156-5

Produced for Bloomsbury Publishing Plc by Sophie Contento
Printed and bound in India

Contents

Acknowledgments

I would like to thank family, friends and colleagues for all their care and support during the writing of this book and the Faculty of Arts and Humanities at the University of East Anglia, who provided a semester's research leave during which I was able to complete it. Thanks also to Charles Drazin and Thoko Mavolwane at Film Finances, who kindly facilitated access to their indispensable archive (which continues to offer the very best in archival refreshments), and the desk staff at the BFI Reuben Library, who were characteristically helpful. Further thanks go to all my editorial contacts at Bloomsbury, Anna Coatman, Veidehi Hans and Rebecca Barden, and to Sophie Contento, who have been unfailingly supportive, patient and sympathetic throughout the project's longer than expected gestation. I would also like to mention the Women's Film and Television History Network, UK/Ireland, and the Paul Mellon Centre for Studies in British Art for providing me with opportunities to present conference papers based on work in progress, helping me to sharpen my ideas. Due to the Covid pandemic, it has not been possible to talk to all the people or undertake all the research that I had originally planned, nor was I able to complete this book to tie in with the sixtieth anniversary of the film's UK release, as initially envisaged. But no matter: since *A Taste of Honey* is partly a film about acceptance and making the best of things, it seems appropriate to adopt a similar attitude in writing about it.

Introduction

If you wanted to get some sense of the zeitgeist of Britain around 1961, you could do worse than watch *A Taste of Honey*.[1] The film is absolutely steeped in its watershed historical moment: a product of the innovative British New Wave in cinema, derived from a play central to postwar theatre's proletarian revolution, imbued with a particular youthful Northern non-conformist sensibility (and with a Liverpudlian star) just one year ahead of The Beatles' first hit record 'Love Me Do'. Indeed, The Beatles would go on to cover the wistful ballad composed for the play's Broadway production, 'A Taste of Honey', on their debut album, the song having been a favourite in their Hamburg repertoire.[2] Appearing on the cusp of the Swinging Sixties but before any swinging had begun in earnest, *A Taste of Honey* dealt with some of the period's most urgent social concerns, from unmarried motherhood to interracial relationships to homosexuality, which certainly didn't harm its commercial prospects: 'Teenage sex, a black baby on the way and a queer boyfriend. She's not so dumb,' observed one Theatre Workshop associate when 18-year-old Shelagh Delaney's roughly typed playscript first arrived through their letterbox in 1958.[3] Film critic Eve Perrick even suspected that

back home in her Salford council house, Miss Delaney had one of those electronic playmaking machines. Into this she fed the most singled-out for discussion topics ... pressed the button marked 'Northern industrial-class accent' – and, lo and behold, out came *A Taste of Honey*.[4]

But although some thought that Delaney's play was contrived, others immediately recognised it as innovative and unique, including influential theatre critic Kenneth Tynan, who praised the teenage playwright for bringing 'real people onto the stage, joking and flaring and scuffling', hailing her as 'a portent', the shape of things to come for British drama.[5]

Released in 1961, Delaney's screen adaptation of her play took its place among a group of realist films emerging in Britain in the late 1950s and early 1960s, soon labelled a 'British New Wave' with reference to France's nouvelle vague. Mostly made by independent production companies such as Woodfall, Romulus and Vic Films, the British New Wave films drew inspiration and source material from working-class novelists and dramatists as well as from the Free Cinema documentary movement in which many of its film-makers (Karel Reisz, Lindsay Anderson and *A Taste of Honey*'s director, Tony Richardson) had participated. Although there had, of course, been previous realist movements in British cinema, this cycle of films instigated by the success of *Room at the Top* (1958) and then followed up by further investigations of Northern working-class life, *Saturday Night and Sunday Morning* (1960), *A Kind of Loving* (1962), *The Loneliness of the Long Distance Runner* (1962), *This Sporting Life* (1963) and *Billy Liar* (1963), was viewed as a crucial postwar breakthrough, challenging the anodyne representations that preceded them and launching new stars proud of their proletarian origins rather than having them elocuted out of existence. However, some were more circumspect in their enthusiasm. For instance, V. F. Perkins in *Movie* magazine queried just how new this New Wave really was in comparison with what had gone before, concluding dismissively:

There is as much genuine personality in *Room at the Top*, method in *A Kind of Loving* and style in *A Taste of Honey* as there is wit in *An Alligator Named Daisy*, intelligence in *Above Us the Waves* and ambition in *Ramsbottom Rides Again*.[6]

Meanwhile, satirical magazine *Private Eye* took aim at middle-class film-makers gushing about 'the raw material of a really down-to-earth portrayal of life as it is actually lived in the North of England'

and creating photogenic visions of 'the smoke and the squalid terraces' before hastily retreating to their smart London addresses once filming was over.[7] Such opinions proved lastingly damning, creating an ongoing ambivalence towards the films within British cinema studies (which is one of the issues this book will explore).

While part of the movement, Woodfall's *A Taste of Honey* was notably different from its New Wave peers, as Anthony Aldgate noted, because 'its concerns were female-centred' and 'women were the instigators of its dramatic action', whereas the protagonists of the other films were young working-class men whose heterosexual desires usually drove the narrative.[8] Many of the New Wave's recurrent thematic concerns would be refracted quite differently in *A Taste of Honey* due to its feminine focus. For example, the usual motif of men's entrapment by women, often through unplanned pregnancies, is upended, with the focus shifted instead to pregnant teenager Jo's own feelings of entrapment and resistance to the expectations of femininity, specifically the maternal identity deemed to be her 'natural' destiny. Also placed centre stage is Jo's fraught push-and-pull relationship with her mother, Helen, who is as resistant as her daughter to maternal expectations, refusing to prioritise Jo above her (sometimes lucrative) romantic relationships. A world away from the diligent desexualised 'our mam' of Richard Hoggart's evocation of Northern working-class respectability in *The Uses of Literacy*, Helen is out for a good time just as much as Arthur Seaton in *Saturday Night and Sunday Morning*.[9] But as a 40-year-old woman rather than a 20-year-old man, she perhaps posed a greater representational challenge within postwar British culture, especially since Delaney refuses to demonise the character (while equally resisting the temptation to sentimentalise her). The film also marked a departure from New Wave norms in foregrounding masculine types generally marginalised by the white heteronormativity which predominated, through the key characters of Jo's Black boyfriend Jimmy and her gay best friend Geoff. Sue Harper argues that *A Taste of Honey* creates 'a utopia in which the outcasts – blacks, homosexuals, tarts – are at the heart of society', daring to

offer female characters 'on the periphery' of social acceptability
who are nonetheless presented as 'anybody's equal'.[10] Mother and
daughter are linked by their ambition for more from life than they are
expected to desire or deserve. The Old Testament allusion in the title
(Jonathan's admission 'I did but taste a little honey with the end of the
rod that was in mine hand, and, lo, I must die') suggests the inevitable
punishment that seems to follow even the most minor infractions
or meagre pleasures. But just as the biblical Jonathan lived to fight
another day despite inadvertently breaking the rules, so Jo and Helen
go on living despite the challenges they face.

That sense of endurance comes through largely via Shelagh
Delaney's distinctive tone as a writer, aptly summarised by Alec
Patton as 'flat declarative sentences, the sarcasm, the epigrammatic
turns of phrase, the stubborn confidence that suddenly dives into
self doubt'.[11] Delaney took exception to the stereotype of deferent
'gormless' working-class Northerners in drama, countering it with
something she felt was more faithful to her 'very alive and cynical'
friends and neighbours in Salford.[12] 'I write how people talk' would
be the young writer's own defence of her sardonic and occasionally
baroque style of Lancastrian dialogue, anticipating and inspiring
the work of subsequent writers from the same region, from Tony
Warren to Victoria Wood, Jeanette Winterson to Delaney mega-fan
Morrissey.[13] But to many critics it seemed unbelievable that a young
working-class woman could ever be the progenitor of such rich
dramaturgy, and just as theatre critics had been quick to surmise
that Delaney had merely provided raw material that had then been
transfigured into a play, film critics similarly assumed that the
alchemy of successful screen adaptation must have been achieved
more by director Tony Richardson than by Delaney: 'the main credit
for this goes to Richardson, who once again reveals a distinct and
unmistakable sense of style'; 'I ascribe the film to him rather than to
Shelagh Delaney'; 'the film's real heroes are Mr Richardson and his
masterly cameraman Walter Lassally'.[14] But as the first actor to play
Jo, Frances Cuka, observed, even though Delaney's play underwent

extensive reworking as part of Theatre Workshop's production process, and lots of people contributed to that, 'the best bits were hers [Delaney's]'.[15] With Cuka's comment in mind, I intend to reinscribe Delaney back into the considerable achievement represented by the film of *A Taste of Honey* and suggest that, again, some of its 'best bits' were 'hers'. While final screenplay credit was shared with Tony Richardson, Delaney's solo-authored first draft screenplay, held in the Film Finances archive, is actually remarkably close to the final version that ended up on screen.[16] In accord with Lavinia Brydon's observation that 'within film scholarship Delaney's talent continues to be overlooked', this book will centre *her* creative contribution to one of the key films of an especially exciting moment in British cinema, and position Delaney as at least as much a female pioneer of postwar British cinema as of theatre.[17] But my account of the film will encompass fully all its myriad innovations, from being shot entirely on location at Richardson's behest, the first modern British mainstream film to do so, to its highly inventive cinematography by Walter Lassally that helped usher in a whole new visual style for British films, to the new kind of screen femininity eloquently embodied by its star discovery Rita Tushingham.[18]

This study explores *A Taste of Honey* as a film in its own right: inevitably tethered to its origins in a hit play and its place within the British New Wave but not limited solely to those interpretative contexts, which have sometimes proved a hindrance to open-minded analysis. Peter Hutchings noted a critical tendency 'to overstress the cohesiveness of the New Wave films' and discuss them en masse, despite their being 'in certain respects quite different from each other'.[19] Partially disaggregating *A Taste of Honey* from those contexts allows for its individuality beyond a group identity to be recognised, yielding new insights.

The book begins with an account of the collective 'hive mind' who contributed to the film's creation and details its production, drawing extensively on archival materials. It then moves into analysis of the first part of the film, detailing Jo's relationship to

home and school and romance. This is followed by a closer look at
the contested meanings of the film's evocation of place and use of
landscape, focusing particularly on Shelagh Delaney's investment
in that aspect; this chapter makes an important intervention into
foundational critical debates on aesthetics and authorship in relation
to British film realism. The next chapter analyses the second half of
the film, covering the consequences of Jo's 'taste of honey' and how
she comes to terms with her situation and forges new allegiances.
A short concluding chapter explores the film's legacies, touching on
its positioning as both cult text and object of nostalgia. Throughout
the book, I simultaneously situate *A Taste of Honey* as very much a
film of 1961, fully inhabiting and expressing its moment of nascent
social and cultural change, but also a 'film classic', as this series
proposes, which speaks eloquently beyond its immediate historical
context. We might characterise this story of youthful dreams,
desires, fears and friendships as a very well-preserved honey, with a
distinctive bittersweet flavour that continues to pique appetites.
This book provides some tasting notes.

1 Hive Mind: Origins and Production of the Film

'Never underestimate 18-year-old girls', Shelagh Delaney warned readers of the *New York Times* in 1961.[20] At precisely that age, she had written and sent off the play that would make her name. And at that same age a few years later, Rita Tushingham was being auditioned for and then cast as Delaney's schoolgirl heroine for the film. Although a great many contributors played their part in realising *A Taste of Honey* on screen (as this chapter makes clear), it is worth noting how remarkable the film was in having at its creative core two young women barely out of their teens, one as screenwriter, one as performer, both of whom were making their debuts within that medium. Furthermore, both represented an emergent mode of femininity that was not prettily deferential but was instead spiky, sarky and demotic. Delaney acknowledged their kinship when she interviewed Tushingham in 1962 for an article: '"What's it like to be a success overnight?" I asked her. "You ought to know", she replied. "I do know, but I'm enjoying asking the question instead of answering it."'[21] As Delaney's comeback suggests, it wasn't always much fun being on the receiving end of intense media scrutiny and constructed as a curiosity. Her short story 'All About and To a Female Artist', a startling verbatim compendium of condescending reviews, begging letters and hate mail, leaves the reader in little doubt about what it feels like to be the recipient of people's envy, snobbery and misogyny, and demonstrates how young women deemed to have overstepped the boundaries of propriety become the locus of others' dark thoughts.[22]

From the very start of her career, Delaney had tried to control the narrative about herself. She'd indulged in some strategic self-fashioning, emphasising her Irish familial heritage by changing the spelling of her first name from Sheila to Shelagh, and shrewdly optimising her status as untutored raw talent when she first wrote her letter of application to Joan Littlewood, appended to her play:

A fortnight ago I didn't know the theatre existed but a young man, anxious to improve my mind, took me along to the Opera House in Manchester and I came away after the performance having suddenly realised that at last, after nineteen years of life, I had discovered something that means more to me than myself ... I set to and produced this little epic – don't ask me why – I'm quite unqualified for anything like this.[23]

In actual fact Delaney was a regular theatregoer who had already been inspired by *Waiting for Godot* and harboured a long-standing desire to write. She had targeted Littlewood specifically because of the theatre director's willingness to work with novice writers and to do battle with the censors, not to mention her pre-existing connections to Salford (where Theatre Workshop had started out). Littlewood was absolutely the ideal target for Delaney's supplicatory salvo, carefully selected as such, and the young writer's ingénue strategy paid off: Littlewood wrote back agreeing to mentor her and produce the play. But Joan Littlewood was no dupe. A savvy promoter, she knew how to maximise the piquant audacity of her new protégée's backstory; indeed, fellow playwright Brendan Behan once remarked that both he and Delaney were 'creations of Joan Littlewood's imagination', carefully crafted attention-grabbing public personae.[24] The press loved the story of Delaney's teenage chutzpah in being bored by Terence Rattigan's play *Variation on a Theme* and aiming to outdo him: 'the redoubtable Salford girl decided she could do better than that'; 'When she came out she said: "I think I could write a play". And she did.'[25] *A Taste of Honey*'s success on its debut in May 1958 at Theatre Workshop's Stratford East base led to a West End transfer in February 1959, where it ran for nearly a year. Delaney won the Foyle's New Play Award, received an Arts Council bursary and was gifted a new typewriter by Graham Greene. But acclaim was far from unanimous. Alan Brien of *The Spectator* (incidentally a friend of Rattigan) dismissed her work as jejune juvenilia: 'Even five years ago, before a senile society began to fawn upon the youth which is about to devour it, such a play would have remained written in green longhand in a school exercise book on the top of the bedroom wardrobe.'[26] If it had any value, it was purely anthropological, as 'the inside story of a savage culture observed by a genuine cannibal'.[27]

The development of Delaney's authorial reputation was accompanied by a growing celebrity clamour around her that revelled in her novelty value. Although numerous other youthful wunderkinds were at work in the artistic milieu of 1950s Britain, such as Angry Young Man Colin Wilson, who'd slept rough while writing his book *The Outsider*, there were hardly any women among their ranks, and even fewer who were working class *and* still in their teens like Shelagh Delaney. Trying to make cultural sense of her, the usual recourse was to a parallel 1950s media sensation, young French author Françoise Sagan, but Sagan's privileged Côte d'Azur lifestyle was some distance from the Salford streets that had nurtured Delaney.

While the British media warily admired her audacity and success, they also fretted incessantly over Shelagh Delaney. They worried about how a young girl could write knowledgably about a situation and a milieu so 'sordid' (the word used most frequently, along with squalid, to describe her play). They took exception to her scruffy beatnik appearance and even her height, sometimes misogynistically combining the two, describing her as resembling ungainly comic actor Bernard Bresslaw when 'observed lumbering through the grey wastes of Stratford, E15, in windcheater and jeans'.[28] They struggled to position her within the conventional gender scripts of the period, and she in turn put up stubborn resistance to what she perceived as their asinine questions: 'No, I don't think I'm an ordinary girl. Does anybody think they're ordinary?' and 'No, I'm not engaged yet' – as though marrying her off would make her a less troublesome figure.[29] Trying to solve the cultural problem she presented, they strove to turn the 'Lancashire tomboy' into a modern Cinderella (with Joan Littlewood as her Fairy

Godmother), as on the occasion of her play's opening night in the West End when she 'cast aside her kneelength slacks and sloppy-Joe sweater, and walked into the foyer of Wyndham's Theatre last night in a glittering white grosgrain dress and silver slippers. ... Shelagh was quite transformed. Those silver slippers were a symbol.'[30] Suffice to say, the premieres of plays by her male contemporaries Arnold Wesker and John Osborne were never covered in quite the same manner.[31]

Back in Salford, the local press worried specifically about the impression Delaney was giving of her hometown, and thus began a long-running antagonism between the writer and her city of origin. Chief orchestrator of what would amount to a press vendetta against Delaney was the editor of the *Salford City Reporter* Saul Reece, who oversaw critical headlines like 'A taste of cash for Shelagh but a kick in the teeth for Salford'.[32] Far from seeing her play as fresh or eye-opening, angry civic dignitaries perceived it as a condescending caricature presented for the edification of snobbish Southerners (not helped by comments like Alan Brien's about cannibals). Delaney was insufficiently humble or homespun to please the city fathers, but as biographer John Harding suggests, that experience of 'being vilified in print, accused of exploiting her hometown for cash' and having 'her talents and achievement openly queried' when she was barely out of her teens undoubtedly left its scars, prompting a recurrent return to the theme of unhappy exilic homecoming in her later films *The White Bus* (1967) and *Charlie Bubbles* (1968).[33]

Delaney was an especially troubling figure in relation to money, as a working-class girl suddenly in possession of a fortune, and as such her celebrity echoed contemporary concerns about growing affluence and responsible consumerism, particularly among the supposedly more suggestible demographic of young women. Newspapers loved reiterating how much money Delaney was reputedly making, fuelling excitable pun-ridden headlines about 'Shelagh's taste of money'.[34] Would she responsibly invest her suddenly burgeoning wealth, the media enquired: her confessions – 'I'm very attracted to luxury. I've developed a taste for orange curacao. And I'd like a big, fast car' – did little to allay fears, while her alleged vow to 'Spend, spend, spend. Quickly, rashly' pre-empted Pools winner Viv Nicholson's notorious statement of intent.[35] In *The Uses of Literacy* Richard Hoggart worried whether 'the idea of "'avin a good time while y'can" because life is hard' might lead to damaging 'soft mass-hedonism' among the working class.[36] Shelagh Delaney, in both word and deed, refuted any such puritanism, passionately defending young women's right to 'raise, sometimes on a grand scale, merry hell':

They drink. They dance. They sing. They LIVE. They mix freely with boys. They spend quickly what money they have in spite of advice to be thrifty and save for the future. For what future? The answer to this question is not as speedily given as the advice that sparked it off. 'Settle down. Settle down. Settle down.' The cry goes up and the criers looked hurt and confess themselves puzzled when the cry is ignored.[37]

Delaney, like girls in general around this time, was expected to walk a tightrope of feminine probity, to be amiable without being a dissipated pleasure-seeker, to spend enough to be appropriately glamorous but without seeming inappropriately acquisitive or self-indulgent, and ultimately to 'settle down'; in short, only a taste of honey was permissible, not the whole pot.

Her desire for the finer things in life also brought her into conflict with her Theatre Workshop mentors, who, as trustees of her earnings until she reached the age of majority at 21, attempted to veto her purchase of the aforementioned 'big, fast car'. Delaney protested furiously to Theatre Workshop's business manager Gerry Raffles:

I've never liked being told what to do and I've no intentions of starting to like it now. You have no right to order me about like some Industrial Revolution employer. ... I've been offered a lot of money for the film rights of my play and I want that car.[38]

And therefore, despite Joan Littlewood being 'the most valuable person I've ever met, as far as work's concerned', Delaney's desire for self-determination (coupled with perhaps a dash of youthful arrogance) meant that she parted company with Theatre Workshop.[39] Her 'difficult' second play, the ambitious ensemble piece *The Lion in Love* (1960), debuted instead at the Belgrade Theatre, Coventry, and after a short national tour (to markedly less critical acclaim than *A Taste of Honey* had received), it transferred to London for a run at the Royal Court theatre, home to the English Stage Company, Theatre Workshop's great rival and main competitor for the status of revolutionary powerhouse in 1950s British theatre, having put on the game-changing *Look Back in Anger* in 1956. Their co-founder and main director was Tony Richardson, who greatly admired Delaney's work and had agreed to direct the New York production of *A Taste of Honey* specifically to leverage support for a screen adaptation to be made by his film company Woodfall. An element of one-upmanship over Theatre Workshop may also have figured; Richardson suggested that the Brechtian badinage of Littlewood's production had trampled over the subtleties of Delaney's 'beautiful play'.[40] His softer approach saw him casting Joan Plowright and Angela Lansbury as the female principals in place of the harsher Frances Cuka and Avis Bunnage, and emphasising the romance between Jo and Jimmy, entailing the composition of the titular ballad 'A Taste of Honey' that would become a hit record. The production 'drew theatregoers like flies' and went on to win the New York Drama Critics' Circle award for Best Foreign Play as well as a Tony award for Plowright.[41]

Around this time, Tony Richardson was best known and most admired as a man of the theatre but always saw this as a means to an end: 'I was going to be a film director, and the way to start was in the theatre'.[42] A founder member of Free Cinema back in the mid-1950s, alongside Karel Reisz and Lindsay Anderson, he was fully signed up to their manifesto statements insisting that 'perfection is not an aim', an approach in evidence in Richardson and Reisz's co-directed short documentary on trad jazz fandom *Momma Don't Allow* (1956).

With the creation of Woodfall, co-founded with John Osborne and Harry Saltzman in 1958, Richardson hoped 'to get into British films the same sort of impact and sense of life that, what you can loosely call the Angry Young Man cult, has had in the theatre and literary worlds', which he deemed 'a desperate need' because of the domestic industry's 'timidity'.[43] He noted how British film production kept 'clinging to the easiest and most conventional ways of doing things. It extends into every department with a mollusc-like tenacity … There is constantly a premium on "this was the way it was done last time" rather than on "this is the way it has never been done".'[44] Saltzman confirmed Richardson's vision of a moribund film establishment which would not only 'not accommodate new creative ideas' but had 'an almost pathological fear of them'.[45] On the company's first two productions, film versions of Osborne's plays, *Look Back in Anger* (1959) and *The Entertainer* (1960), Richardson found himself forced to compromise between the conventional modus operandi of mainstream production (glossy cinematography, studio sets, star casting) and the more neorealist-influenced style of film-making that he wanted to pursue. Both films would achieve only a modicum of critical acclaim and neither were box-office triumphs, despite having star performances from Richard Burton and Laurence Olivier respectively (or perhaps because of this, Richardson would later surmise).

Through making his first few films, Richardson learned a lot about what he didn't want to do in film-making, and wasn't afraid to voice his opinions: as a later profile suggested, his apparently 'languid air' was 'misleading. Beneath the drawl and the hesitations there lies the hard knot of self-recognition.'[46] Echoing the Free Cinema manifesto, Richardson stated there was no point striving for 'technical perfection' because 'we all know this doesn't matter a tiny damn … Gloss guarantees nothing.'[47] Filming in studios offered control, but it was empty in comparison with more serendipitous on-the-spot shooting: 'miracles happen on location which you could never conceive of or imagine when you are writing the script. Life is

Directing in a dingy flat complete with plate-rack over the bathtub: Dora Bryan and Tony Richardson

always more daring and extravagant than art.'[48] This was in 1959; by the following year he was even more emphatic: 'I hate studios. I no longer want to shoot even interiors in a studio. I would rather work in the limited conditions which a location imposes upon you.'[49] Put more simply, his realist credo was 'If I want a scene in a dingy flat, I'll find a dingy flat and shoot there.'[50]

Richardson's brief and largely disastrous sojourn in Hollywood making *Sanctuary* (1961) for Twentieth Century-Fox had convinced him that it was 'impossible to make anything that is interesting or good under the conditions imposed by the major studios in America'.[51] But for a time it looked as though securing finance to make *A Taste of Honey* would entail a dance with that particular devil. Daryl Zanuck at Fox was interested in the project but demanded major alterations to make the project commercially viable in his eyes, which included casting Audrey Hepburn as Jo, and ensuring the film had a 'happy' ending, although Zanuck's idea of happiness was highly questionable: 'the baby's gotta die, and the mother and girl go off to a better life'.[52] To make matters worse, Harry Saltzman back at Woodfall largely shared Zanuck's view, regarding the project as 'too provincial and too English' with 'little appeal or popular identification for people in other countries. As I saw it, the film should have been set in France, with Simone Signoret as the mother and Leslie Caron as the girl, which would've made it into an international picture.'[53] Saltzman's attempts to sell on the rights without Richardson's consent became a major bone of contention between them, and one of the factors triggering his departure from Woodfall; ever the commercial-minded showman, Saltzman immediately went on to co-create Eon, the production company behind the James Bond film franchise, placing himself at the centre of another foundational moment in 1960s British cinema.

But before Saltzman's departure, Woodfall's fortunes had dramatically changed anyway in 1960 with the huge popularity of Karel Reisz's film *Saturday Night and Sunday Morning*, which made a star of Albert Finney and became one of the biggest British box-office hits of the year. Bringing the money rolling in to Woodfall's coffers, it also triumphantly vindicated the company's unorthodox approach to film-making: an unknown lead, debut director and controversial subject matter, all usually indicators of box-office poison, but a huge hit nonetheless. It consolidated *Room at the Top*'s previous successful challenge to conventional wisdom, further proving a strong public appetite for realist tales of working-class Northern life if told in appealing ways.

A Taste of Honey would also benefit from the support of completion guarantee company Film Finances, who were 'instrumental in giving untried directors and actors a chance' and 'funding largely location-based projects', which, as Sarah Street notes, made them unsung heroes in facilitating this moment of change in British films.[54] Although not to assessor John Croydon's taste ('a story

sordid in the extreme, and one for which I do not particularly care'),
he recognised its viability as a project and recommended that Film
Finances support it.[55] It helped that Croydon had already worked
extensively with Richardson and could vouch for him:

In many ways the whole thing – story, script, and method of production –
defies convention, and I think, from our point of view, that our consideration
of these papers must be determined by the extent to which we are prepared
to go along with him. My own experience of him – on The Entertainer – tells
me that Richardson is a hard worker with a basic sense of responsibility.[56]

Croydon provided reassurance that, although an all-location
production was somewhat unorthodox, it was perfectly possible
'provided the task is tackled realistically and sensibly', and Richardson
had someone 'prepared to jog his elbow from time to time'.[57]

Backing from Film Finances and the boost provided by *Saturday
Night and Sunday Morning*'s success enabled Tony Richardson to
make *A Taste of Honey* in the way that he wanted. But its bedrock
would be Shelagh Delaney's script. She had signed a contract with
Woodfall setting out her agreement 'to write a first draft screenplay
(hereinafter called "the draft screenplay") suitable for the shooting
of a first feature film based on the Writer's play', and delivered the
first version on 22 February 1960, going on to make further minor
revisions to the draft dated 16 April 1960.[58] Both versions of the
screenplay are credited solely to Delaney. Although Richardson had
told Croydon 'that the script should be read with discretion as it
was his intention to adapt the content of the scenes to the chosen
locations', in actual fact very few substantive changes were made to
what Delaney had initially supplied, as Croydon himself noted in a
letter of 7 February 1961: 'We are dealing with the same script ...
the fact that the schedule refers to selected sites will make little or
no difference to the scene content.'[59] With the benefit of a few years'
work and life experience after its theatrical debut, Delaney had deftly
adapted her own play, turning it into something new but still faithful

to her preoccupations and passions, which were themselves evolving during her early twenties. She answered the call of the cinematic that her play had arguably been straining towards from its inception, as Joan Littlewood had suggested in reference to its opening stage directions: 'A section of a street, the main entrance to a house, a living-room with two doors and a window overlooking the river, a bedroom, a kitchen. It needed a film unit.'[60] Littlewood had brought the play within the confines of feasible dramatic staging. But the film would extrapolate it back into real locations, many of them deeply familiar to Delaney as childhood haunts and hometown landmarks.

Tony Richardson's stated objective with *A Taste of Honey* was 'to force a much rougher style on the film, and to force myself to shoot in, I hope, a freer way'.[61] To achieve this, he needed the right crew. Croydon felt Richardson was 'a man who cannot afford to work with inferior technicians, or men without imagination'.[62] Thankfully, this was never a problem for Richardson, who was a superb gatherer and galvaniser of talent, with Karel Reisz praising his 'confidence and impresario genius', which empowered his collaborators: 'His attitude was "You have a go".'[63] He nurtured and encouraged new talent, such as future Woodfall directors Desmond Davis (camera operator on *A Taste of Honey*) and Peter Yates (its first assistant director) or a brilliant young editor like Antony Gibbs, who would go from strength to strength on subsequent Woodfall films. But equally, experienced personnel were offered an opportunity to experiment with their craft, exemplified by art director Ralph Brinton, an industry veteran enjoying a second wind in his career through his association with the British New Wave.[64] Brinton was in complete accord with Richardson's views on location filming's 'feeling of spontaneity', which was 'difficult to create consciously in the studio':

the desire for perfection in each department had led to the 'tyranny of expertise' ... which can easily defeat its own object and stifle the freedom and originality of the director ... The inevitable limitations of a location go a long way to redress the balance against such restrictive perfectionism ...

less preoccupation with the perfectionism of set design, lighting and sound may well result in less inhibiting conditions of work and so help produce the true realism which we are seeking.[65]

Other sympathetic veterans on the team included Sophie Devine of the Motley design team, whose career stretched back into the 1930s, overseeing wardrobe with Barbara Gillett, and composer John Addison, who had scored numerous British films since 1950, but whose association with Woodfall and Richardson would prove especially fruitful, resulting in an Oscar for *Tom Jones* (1963).[66]

Where Richardson had been assigned classically inclined cinematographer Oswald Morris as a guarantor of professional polish on his Osborne adaptations, for this project he was able to choose a director of photography and brought in his old Free Cinema colleague Walter Lassally, previously vetoed due to industry inexperience beyond documentary work. Lassally's edgier, improvisational approach was ideally suited to capturing the happy accidents of location shooting and the rougher aesthetic Richardson wanted. Testing the limits of what was possible creatively, Lassally planned to move between three film stocks of varying grain in different sections of the film, 'including the high-speed (400 ASA) material, Ilford HPS, hitherto considered suitable only for newsreels and documentaries', and 'to "key" the use of these different film stocks to different locations, so that the "look" they created became part of the setting'.[67] Warned against its potentially jarring effect by the processing laboratories, Woodfall would end up having to use a lab more used to handling non-commercial film to get the desired finish. The use of high-speed Ilford film, which could cope with lower light levels without major deterioration in image quality, also enabled Lassally to work extensively with diegetic light sources, only minimally augmented (mainly by reflectors), creating a realist look which nonetheless possessed 'romantic and lyrical' qualities.[68] He used real-life low light in highly expressive fashion, from dancehall twinkle to bonfire flames, late-night lamplight to watery Mancunian

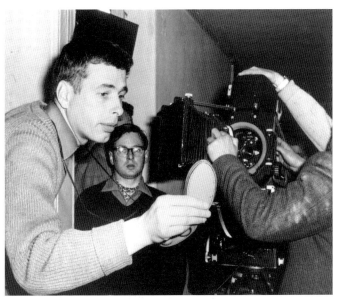

Cinematographer Walter Lassally at work, and a moment of lamplit lyricism

sunshine, and even managed to photograph a scene lit solely by
candlelight – and in a dark cave too – more than a decade before
Kubrick's *Barry Lyndon* (1975).

Another vital component of Woodfall's modus operandi was
its desire to cast fresh faces in starring roles rather than relying on
established stars, a tactic that had worked magnificently well with
Albert Finney. When it came to the lead role of Jo in *A Taste of
Honey*, Richardson felt that stage actors Frances Cuka and Joan
Plowright were both too old to be convincing screen teenagers, but
also had to be mindful of BBFC advice to avoid 'a "Lolita element"'
by not casting too young.[69] On the basis of his enjoyment of 'working
with people who are doing their first film', finding 'newcomers more
spontaneous', Woodfall decided to launch an open audition process.[70]
As reported in the press, their requirements were unusual, almost the
antithesis of Selznick's famous search for his Scarlett O'Hara:

Tony Richardson began what must surely be the most curious quest of the
week: the search for an ugly, unknown actress to star in the film version of
Miss Delaney's hit play, 'A Taste of Honey.' ... The search is fascinating, for it is
all part of the new pattern in British picture-making – the trend towards vivid
realism ... Explained Richardson: 'The whole film really depends on the impact
of this girl. The audience has to be made to believe that it is really watching Jo,
a Salford teenager, and there isn't a star in Britain who could play the part.'[71]

Having interviewed and auditioned hundreds of young actors
(including a young Judi Dench), by April 1960 they had finally found
their Jo: 18-year-old Rita Tushingham, a lowly trainee assistant stage
manager at the Liverpool Playhouse and aspiring actress with only
limited stage experience.[72] Tushingham's first audition initially left
Richardson feeling 'she was too fierce, too spiky, too hard-edged'.[73]
But, he later recalled, 'that little hedgehog from Liverpool haunted
me in some way' and a screen test finally sealed the deal: 'a close-up
of Rita with her all-speaking eyes was on the screen, and the search
was over'.[74]

'You don't know this girl …': introducing Rita Tushingham

Tushingham's discovery was presented under the unflattering headline 'Found: the ugly girl (once she was the hind legs of a donkey)' in the *Daily Express*, while the *People* declared her 'a star overnight because of her cute little ugly mug!' (John Osborne countered that she had 'more expression and beauty when she crooks her little finger than most of those damned starlets will ever have – even if they waggle their oversized bosoms and bottoms from here to eternity').[75] The Cinderella makeover motif previously foisted onto Delaney was now applied to Tushingham, another young woman deemed to not quite fit the usual mould of feminine fame. 'Rita of Liverpool' had 'crooked teeth, rough hair and a plain nose on her face', according to the *Daily Mirror*'s Marje Proops, but she concluded that, nonetheless, in her 'off-the-peg blue chiffon dress' bought for the premiere:

tomorrow night Rita will be a film star – sometimes dreams DO come true. The homely girl next door CAN wake up one day to find the fame she's dreamed about is within her reach. Carry on dreaming, girls. It happened to Rita Tushingham. It could happen to you.[76]

Tushingham's ordinariness was emphasised in publicity and press coverage ('The overnight wonder shuns sophistication [and] has no pretensions', the pressbook boasted), including the retention of her original name rather than a starrier-sounding substitute.[77] Although opinion was divided on whether Woodfall's new discovery was ordinary or extraordinary, homely or beautiful, the company simply asked exhibitors to trust their track record in spotting future stars: 'You don't know this girl …' declared their ad in the trade press next to a publicity shot of Tushingham, and overleaf there was a grinning Albert Finney captioned 'but you know him'.[78]

Richardson's preference for working with newcomers extended to other members of the cast. Murray Melvin had played the role of Geoffrey, Jo's gay friend and flatmate, since its Theatre Workshop origination and throughout its West End run (and was the only member of any stage production to be cast in the film) so thus was an old hand in the role but a new face ('extraordinary … like an Egyptian hieroglyph', according to Richardson) in films.[79] Paul Danquah, cast as Jo's boyfriend Jimmy, was a total newcomer not

The hieroglyphic-featured Murray Melvin as Geoff

Fresh face: newcomer Paul Danquah as Jimmy

only to films but to acting in general, having embarked on a change of career while studying for the bar (he replaced the earlier casting idea of Billy Dee Williams, who'd played Jimmy on Broadway).[80] Although Richardson spoke of his wish to avoid actors who had 'been used thousands of times, because I think they are like old worn coins that the public don't respond to freshly', the casting of Dora Bryan as Jo's mother, Helen, flew in the face of this logic.[81] A star of revue and variety as well as one of the most familiar figures in British cinema, Bryan had been playing ladies of slightly dubious virtue since *The Fallen Idol* (1948). Her job just prior to *A Taste of Honey* had been twice-nightly summer season in Bournemouth with pop singer Marty Wilde, indicating her firm grounding in popular entertainment that provided a link back to the Theatre Workshop conception of Helen as a music-hall comedienne.[82] The pub singalong

Dora Bryan as Helen leads the pub singalong while Robert Stephens as Peter stands by sheepishly

she confidently leads in the film lets the variety star shine through. And if Richardson had gone along with the initial casting idea of Leslie Phillips playing Helen's fancyman Peter, there would have been further intertextual complexity in terms of an established screen persona, the raffish roué in Phillips' case.[83] But in the end, rising stage star Robert Stephens was cast in the role, 'oozing vulnerability, embarrassment and lechery' very effectively, according to Robert Murphy's later assessment.[84] With that, the main cast was complete.

Shooting began on 14 March 1961 on location on the Manchester Ship Canal. The bulk of filming in Salford, Manchester, Stockport, as well as Blackpool and the Peak District for the daytrips taken by different characters, was completed by early April. Such efficiency was even more impressive given the variable weather conditions they had to contend with, detailed across numerous daily production reports (e.g. 26 March's 'Weather too bad for exterior

A lovefest: laughter during a break in location filming among director and cast

shooting' and 1 April's 'Very bad weather. Rained most of the day').[85] In spite of this, it seems to have been a very upbeat production that Richardson recalled years later as unusually contented: 'Once Rita had been found, everything went wonderfully – a lovefest with both crew and actors', and he recalled feeling 'free and happy making a film for the first time without constraints of any kind'.[86] It seems to have fulfilled his stated ideal for location filming, when 'you go off like gypsies, a band of travellers, focusing all your efforts and indeed your life on making that film, for the period of shooting.'[87]

Production relocated to London on 6 April for shooting interiors, which took place at two sites. One was at 74 Elm Park Gardens, a townhouse off the Fulham Road, which acted as Jo and Helen's shared flat and also functioned as a production base, described evocatively by the *Daily Herald*:

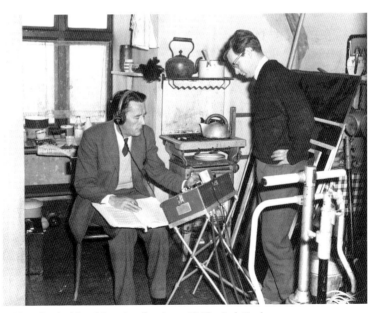

'A hive of technicians': location shooting at 74 Elm Park Gardens

Inside the house is a tangle of cables, a hive of technicians, a chatter of
actresses ... The sound recording department is a nook under the stairs.
Stages Two and Three are in the attic. [The film] is being made in rooms with
real ceilings and walls so the camera cannot swoop, perch overhead, circle
round or do anything much except photograph the acting.[88]

The other site was the Royal Court's prop store and set workshop
in Dixon's Yard near its Sloane Square premises, standing in for Jo's
studio flat with the courtyard below. This section of production
ran as smoothly as the Northern location filming, although it did
entail some long working days and nights to get everything done;

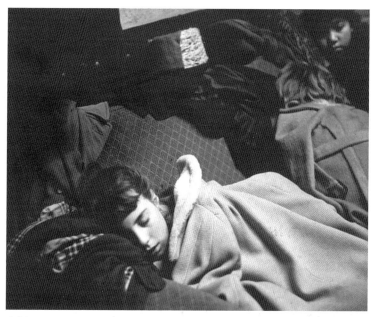

Child extras get some sleep during overnight filming of the bonfire scene

for example, the daily production progress report for 26 April notes how the unit 'worked through night until 4.30 am to complete Bonfire sequence'.[89] The majority of production completed by 28 April, it only remained for a small unit to go back up to Manchester in the final week of May to do some retakes and complete the Whit Week Walks sequence. By then, editing was already underway, and although the first post-production progress report anticipated the final cut being delivered on 31 July 1961, in the end it would be nearer the end of August, just ahead of its mid-September premiere.

The film had a budget of only £120,940, which as a reporter at the time noted was about 'one-twenty-fifth' the original estimate for Fox's *Cleopatra* (1963).[90] But despite the modesty of its provenance, hopes were high for another success for Woodfall, following on from *Saturday Night and Sunday Morning*. Tony Richardson had been able to implement his ideal way of film-making as never before. But he was working with fantastic source material, courtesy of Shelagh Delaney, and as if to signal this debt of gratitude, Delaney has a brief cameo appearance in the film's opening scenes, silently and inscrutably watching over a netball match from the touchlines in her long tweed overcoat. Although other key production personnel have cameos too, including composer John Addison playing pub piano and Tony Richardson walking along Blackpool promenade, it feels fitting that Shelagh Delaney is an unobtrusive but commanding presence from the film's outset, presiding over the first moments of the story that she created and the introduction of the young misfit protagonist she originated back in Salford when she was only a teenager, one remarkable girl overseeing another.

Shelagh take a bow: Delaney in the background during the film's opening scene

2 Into the Film: A Young Woman's Prospects

For anyone who hated school PE, especially the dreaded netball, the opening moments of *A Taste of Honey* are likely to spark chilling recognition of impenetrable rules, continual exhortations to effort and ill-fitting kit. These scenes seem calculated to place many of us in instant sympathy with Jo, enduring 'one of those compulsory periods that all have to submit to' and a 'game she obviously loathes', as Shelagh Delaney described it in her draft screenplay, and hitting out at an approaching (hard) ball in grumpy but ineffectual retaliation (Delaney noted that she wanted this sequence 'treated with a sort of slightly balletic comedy – but not St. Trinian's').[91] These scenes form our initial introduction to Jo, and she is emphatically not a team player. They also introduce Rita Tushingham, the unknown newcomer cast in the film's lead role, an eloquent first close-up of her face picking her out from the rest of the players as she casts an indignant eye over proceedings. Jo will later say, defensively, that she's 'bad on purpose'; this shot conveys some of that attitude of truculent non-compliance.[92]

Jo's difference from her classmates is underlined further when they're all back in the changing room after the final whistle, washing their faces and titivating their hair before home time. Jo can't go out dancing like them because, she says, she doesn't have the right clothes to wear, and in any case a 'moonlight flit' to avoid paying the rent looks likely that evening. Once the rest of them have hurried off to lead their more exciting social lives, she lags behind, washing her face and contemplating her reflection in the mirror, blowing soap bubbles over the sink. The film takes its time over this scene, just as Jo herself is taking her time, and we are treated to rapturous close-ups of Tushingham's protean beauty, by turns awkward then soulful, spiky then soft, as changeable as the Manchester weather. As Robert Shail observes, sometimes 'Richardson seems almost overwhelmed by his fascination with Tushingham, so that the narrative pauses to allow Lassally's camera to contemplate again her quirky, engaging features.'[93]

As Jo returns home from school and descends the stairs into the basement flat she shares with her mother, noises off indicate a disagreement with the landlady over rent arrears and gentleman callers. Jo eavesdrops behind the door before it swings open to reveal her mother, Helen (Dora Bryan), supine on a divan, like a corruption

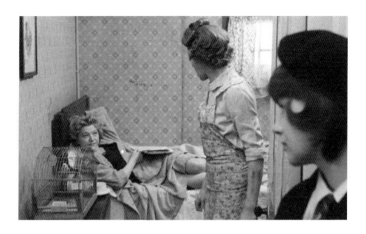

of Manet's Olympia, with the budgerigar in a non-gilded cage hinting at her status as a kept woman, which had been made more explicit in Delaney's play with its mention of 'immoral earnings'. Unlike the reclining silent courtesan of fine art, this one answers back, using her Lancashire burr to dismissively dispatch the nagging landlady: 'Oh shurrup, you'll get your rent.' But Helen is not as good as her word and, as Jo had suspected, a flit ensues, not under cover of darkness but at teatime when the landlady's glued to the telly. Their escape shows how difficult it is to maintain a dignified appearance while squeezing out of a small basement window with several suitcases, a hatbox and a budgie cage, and also while tottering down a steep cobbled slope in high heels and a billowing plastic mac, only precariously upright, literally as well as morally. Helen cuts a highly conspicuous figure in the stolid Lowry-esque landscape of brick terraces, factory chimneys and cobbled streets, embodying 'shiny barbarism' in contrast to the traditional working-class community's 'full rich life', to adopt Richard Hoggart's oppositions.[94] Jo and Helen are out on their own, exiled from all that.

Jo, headscarved and heavily encumbered, troops along behind her mother as they descend to the bus stop, to travel across town and find themselves new lodgings. Their bus journey through the

centre of Manchester provides the backdrop for the film's opening credits, accompanied by a children's choir singing 'The Big Ship Sails on the Alley-Alley-O', variations on which underpin John Addison's entire score. The film crosscuts between the sights Jo and her mother see through the bus windows and their responses to them, telling us about their opposing characters as much as the world they inhabit. While Jo is wide-eyed and inquisitive, taking in everything she sees, her mother sniffs, sneezes and curls her lip.

The monumental Victorian buildings of Manchester's 'Cottonopolis' and the overwhelmingly male civic statuary across the city appear to offer gestures of rebuke to the errant women, underlined by some of the song's lyrics: 'The Captain said it would never, never do.'[95] Helen meets this with a dismissive eyeroll rather than any sense of being truly chastened, suggesting defiance in spite of their alterity.[96] And at least there's a chivalrous fellow passenger who helps them with their suitcases when they reach their destination: Jo's first chance encounter with Jimmy, her future fiancé.

The next scene is where Delaney's original play began, as Jo and Helen enter their new lodgings and start to unpack. There doesn't seem to be much love lost between mother and daughter, with bickering defining their exchanges rather than any obvious affection, a mode of communication that continues throughout the film, with a few rare exceptions. Their disagreements over who should light the stove and make the coffee evoke this sense of habitual verbal antagonism. Its back and forth, thrust and parry, is superbly and often hilariously performed by Bryan and Tushingham. At certain points, there are loud threats of violence ('I'll knock your ruddy head off!'), but they are never acted upon. Instead there seems to be a close bond in their state of perpetual enmity, as Helen later admits when

Mother–daughter antagonism and ambivalence: Jo and Helen

Geoff tries to intervene during one particularly heated argument: 'Oh shut up, we enjoy it.' But their closeness is not sentimentalised, and it is made clear that this is born of penury and is mutually claustrophobic, as Jo longs for a room and a bed of her own, while Helen jokes sarcastically that she 'can't bear to be parted' from her daughter, 'not for a minute'.

Although Jo can be hilariously acerbic to others (her ''Ello Daddy!' to Peter when she finds out Helen is marrying him is a particular highlight), she reserves her sharpest barbs for her mother, casting aspersions on her age, pointing out that she doesn't 'look forty' but more 'a sort of well-preserved sixty', and criticising Helen's attempts at glamour: of a new fur stole, Jo glumly opines, 'Bet somebody's missing their cat.' But Helen refuses to take Jo seriously, acknowledging her rudeness with equanimity: 'I must be a biological phenomenon', 'I know, I'm a cruel, wicked mother.' It's not all snappy banter though, with a darker, sadder edge to many of their interactions. Jo's fear of the dark, 'not the darkness outside but the darkness inside', suggests her loneliness and dread of abandonment, bearing the emotional scars of growing up with a mother who resented caring for her and, according to Jo, always took her hand away when she tried to hold it. There will be two pivotal scenes of hand-holding with the two men in her life (a prelude to her first kiss with Jimmy, and a moment of closeness in the churchyard with Geoff), both conveying a sense of trying to assuage the pain of that first formative rejection.

Terry Lovell suggests that *A Taste of Honey* offers a rare depiction of 'the little girl jealous not of her mother but of her mother's lover, raging against her own neglect', displacing the usual Oedipal drivers of male-focused drama.[97] This emotional dynamic reaches a climax during their later trip to Blackpool, with Jo hurling the accusation 'you've never been affectionate with me!' at her mother. Jo had invited herself along, partly to make a nuisance of herself, partly to make a point, and the clothes she wears, a masquerade of festive femininity recalling Larkin's phrase

'parodies of fashion', accessorised with feathery headband, silk
scarf, corsage, dainty gloves and handbag, and a sullen expression,
underline her mute resistance to being sidelined by her mother's
pursuit of pleasure. Knowing it will antagonise Helen and Peter, the
unloved child feels driven to make herself as undelightful as possible;
just like being deliberately bad at netball as a defence mechanism.
Jo suspects that if forced to choose, Helen will pick her latest lover
over her, and is eventually proved correct when the moment comes,
although she is clearly torn between defending her daughter and
protecting what she feels are her best interests in individualistic terms.
Later on, we see Helen state outright that having a child doesn't
place you under any obligation to it and she often seems to carry
through ruthlessly on this conviction. Critic Paul Dehn noted that
alongside Dora Bryan's humour and 'flair for pathos', there was 'a
sort of glaze that drops over her eyes and eclipses their lovability' in
certain scenes.[98] But in spite of all this there is still a residual mother–
daughter tie that cannot be completely severed and is tentatively
reactivated by the film's close where a kind of comradeship emerges
from Jo repeating the cycle of lone motherhood, despite Helen
explicitly warning against it: 'Oh Jo, why can't you learn from my
mistakes? It takes half your lifetime to learn from your own.'

A *Taste of Honey* expresses considerable ambivalence and complexity around mothering and being mothered, psychic territory absent from the rest of the core canon of the British New Wave. But 'because of the masculine address of this whole group of New Wave films' and 'because *A Taste of Honey* is visually and generically at one with them', Terry Lovell observes, this aspect of the film has often been analytically downplayed.[99] Reframing *A Taste of Honey* as a woman's picture enables better recognition of its generic range and the elements of maternal melodrama and female *Bildungsfilm* that it contains.[100] Rather than being automatically bracketed with its New Wave peers, it might be productively connected with other British films of the early 1960s focused on contemporary female experience and subjectivity, cutting across different genres, such as *Beat Girl* (1960), *Girl on Approval* (1960), *The L-Shaped Room* (1962), *The World Ten Times Over* (1963), *The Pumpkin Eater* (1964) and *Darling* (1965). Viewed in this company, *A Taste of Honey* would appear less anomalous and more like one instance of a wider series of examinations into women's changing lives that British cinema was in the process of undertaking as sexual permissiveness slowly, tentatively, began to unfold.[101]

* * *

A Taste of Honey opens with a kind of ending: Jo's schooldays, and therefore by inference the last vestiges of her childhood, are drawing to a close. The question of what she should do next rears its head. When Helen accidentally spills the contents of Jo's art folder and looks through the portfolio of sketches that fall out, she expresses surprise at her 'talented daughter'. 'I'm not just talented, I'm geniused' is Jo's lugubriously smart alec response, but she firmly resists Helen's suggestion that she might want to continue her education at art college, out of a mixture of pique ('Why are you so suddenly interested in me? You never cared much before') and a genuine wish to be an independent wage-earner as soon as she can. In this age of high employment, the world of work was a more enticing prospect, offering greater personal autonomy. Although Jo could have perhaps embraced her artistic talent and got a grant to go on to art college, wellsprings for social and artistic experimentation from the 1950s onwards (although to a lesser extent for young women then), being disenchanted with any form of 'school' and, for all her bravado about being 'geniused', unsure of herself, the workplace is her destination instead.[102] But before she gets to that point, she must complete her schooling. In addition to seeing Jo grimly enduring PE, we also witness one of her final English lessons. The teacher is reading aloud Keats' 'Ode to a Nightingale' and, in the words of Delaney's screenplay, Jo is 'listening enraptured by the poem, completely caught and spellbound by it'.[103] But her classmates manage to toll her back into mischief, passing a note in an exercise

Artistic, poetic Jo: with her 'geniused' artwork and 'enraptured' by Keats

book and then laughing at Jo's comic mime of extravagant romantic adieus and violin virtuosity. Catching her out mid-mime, the teacher assumes the worse and throws the board rubber at her erring pupil, unaware of her previous rapture. Jo is made to stay behind to write lines, a standard punishment for insubordination but also a deliberate refusal of any creativity on the part of the offender; endless, pointless repetition is what is exacted here.

Jo's poetic enthusiasm goes sadly unnoticed and unnurtured at school. This was a matter of considerable personal concern to Delaney. In her 1960 appearance on the BBC television arts series *Monitor*, discussing life in Salford, she placed great emphasis on the iniquities of a divisive education system from the unusual perspective of someone who had been both a secondary modern and grammar school pupil, transferred from former to latter for her final years of schooling. She knew for herself how both school streams often failed to recognise or develop latent talents. The result was a kind of 'restlessness' among young people, an existential uncertainty about what to do in the world that Delaney knew well:

when I was 17 I was in a terrible mess, I didn't know what to do with myself, I knew I wanted to do something but what? … I was lucky, dead lucky, but so many aren't and that's the tragedy.[104]

Delaney described the collective experience of modern working-class youth in a place such as Salford as being 'like a horse on a tether, jerking about', waiting to be cut free. Her concerns about young people's thwarted potential would have received further elucidation in *A Taste of Honey* via a scene that was scripted and shot but ultimately unused in the film, detailing Jo's interaction with a youth employment officer. It uncannily anticipates a moment from the later Woodfall film *Kes* (1969) in which a school-leaver is presented with depressingly limited choices for his future by an unsympathetic careers advisor. Delaney's draft screenplay describes a 'terrible' room in which 'a row of people sit – none of them over the age of sixteen or seventeen':

Appallingly cold and cheerless with cream distempered walls and tubular steel chairs. There are no curtains at the windows. No flowers on the table. Nothing at all to alleviate the air of gloom and fatefulness that overshadows everything else.[105]

A 'ferocious looking' youth employment officer suggests a position as a greengrocer's assistant, and if she doesn't like that, then there are opportunities in the cardboard box factory, growing impatient with Jo's lack of enthusiasm, while Jo in turn is described as 'getting angrier and angrier as the woman is unable to understand that she wants something but doesn't really know what'.[106] Although not strictly essential, the scene's omission nonetheless feels like a loss in terms of depicting the stark reality of Jo's situation and limited prospects as a working-class school-leaver.[107] Delaney gestures towards a whole cohort of similarly frustrated inarticulate teenagers, herself among them not that long ago, made 'restless' by an educational system she characterised as 'miserable, and without any doubt, wasteful' in its lack of care.[108] There were additional gendered dimensions to being sold short educationally, as Delaney noted:

The idea that time and money spent on thoroughly educating a girl is time and money wasted persists and many girls, if they lack the strength to fight it, often find themselves living and working in a way that bores and frustrates them. They feel cheated of opportunities that have been accorded, as if by some divine right, to the opposite sex. ... the money available is automatically – and usually irrespective of talents – spent on the male child while the female child is let loose with instructions – if not in so many words – to get herself a husband. This act, it is commonly supposed, will solve all her problems.[109]

Once Jo's school has finished with processing her, the building even appears to expel her physically, and with such projectile force that she trips down the steps and badly cuts her knee. But her fall is also the pretext for her 'meet cute' with the boy from the bus,

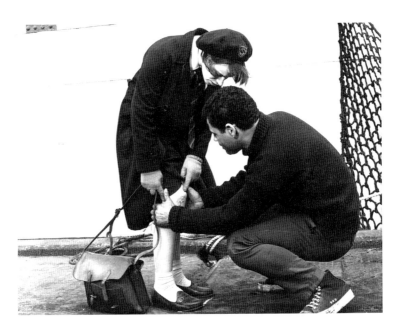

who turns out to be a seaman on a big ship (moored on the canal that Jo walks along on her way home from school) who offers to clean and bandage her cut knee.

Jimmy presents a beguiling alternative to the grind of school and the unpredictability of home, taking an interest in Jo that may have ulterior sexual motives ('I wonder what the thought was in your wicked mind that made you buy it', Jo later jokes when he presents her with an engagement ring) but which does seem sincerely affectionate. Although he does look older than Jo, who wears her school uniform at several of their meetings (and jokes about her 'schoolgirl complexion'), his courtship is ardent without being coercive and he only wants to stay the night, 'If that's what you want.' The couple have fun together, sometimes in a way proximate to childhood games, when they hopscotch along the street or play hide-and-seek, but their relationship isn't infantilised or asexual, as their arch flirtatious banter after their first tryst on Jimmy's ship suggests:

JO   Anything might happen to a girl.

JIMMY   It almost did, you shameless woman.

JO   That's you taking advantage of my innocence.

JIMMY   You enjoyed it as much as I did.

JO   Shut up, this is the sort of conversation that can colour
            a young girl's mind.

Jo professes to love Jimmy because he's 'daft', a word that will garner
bleaker undertones later in the film but here indicates how much
theirs is a bond forged by laughter as well as desire.

The couple's banter engages light-heartedly with tropes of
racial representation, sometimes in ways that sound uncomfortable
to contemporary ears, as with a throwaway reference to the violently
suppressed anti-colonial Mau Mau uprising, but the general

intent is to send up rather than shore up racist stereotypes. Jimmy corrects Jo on her assumptions about his ancestry – he comes from Liverpool rather than 'darkest' Africa – before asking her 'were you expecting to marry a man whose father beat the tom-tom?' and slapping Jo's school satchel in a pastiche of tribal drumming, which Jo then accompanies with an ersatz African dance, retorting: 'There's still a bit of jungle in you somewhere.' A white schoolgirl and a Black sailor could have been seen as an incendiary love match in the conservative climate of the period, more likely to be treated through the auspices of neurotic social problem melodrama, as with *Sapphire* (1959) and *Flame in the Streets* (1961). By comparison Jo and Jimmy's romance is generally presented as carefree, their courtship one of 'unpretentious freshness'.[110] And they are granted the aesthetic benediction of some of Walter Lassally's most beautiful cinematography, such as accompanies their first kiss just as twilight is darkening into night (which dissolves seamlessly into the twinkling starry canopy ceiling of the Ritz Ballroom, thanks to Gibbs' deft editing), or their lingering farewell underneath the lamplight, or perhaps most wrenchingly, their long goodbye after spending their first and only night together when Jimmy has to rejoin his departing ship. He stands semi-silhouetted on the moving swing bridge,

physically separated from Jo by its inexorable movement, while she looks over the barrier and slowly waves goodbye (a genuine heartfelt 'adieu' after the ones she'd pastiched in her English lesson).

The development of Jimmy and Jo's tender romance is contrasted and crosscut with the more frenetic ogling and groping of Helen's relationship with second-hand car salesman Peter. While the younger couple embrace in an urban pastoral of lonely waterways and zigzagging brick steps overlooked by the cylindrical filigree of gas towers, prompting intertextual echoes of Ewan MacColl's Salford ballad 'Dirty Old Town' where love's young dream occurs against a backdrop of gasworks walls and old canals, the older couple are confined indoors, in pubs, dancehalls or narrow, enclosed staircases.[111] The idea of contrived synthetic thrills jump-starting their mature coupling is emphasised, as Helen jives exaggeratedly with Peter at the Ritz Ballroom, all frenzied movement and blur and loud music, contrasting with the quiet placidity of the canal that provides the backdrop for Jo and Jimmy's burgeoning shipboard romance. The Ritz's starry sky is pretty but artificial; Jo and Jimmy have the real thing overhead. Two proposals of marriage are also juxtaposed: Peter's drunken, lustful proposition in a dancefloor clinch and Jimmy's canal-side presentation of a ring that Jo will wear on a

Filming at the Ritz Ballroom

ribbon around her neck in romantic clandestine fashion. Of course Jimmy and Jo's relationship has to be more tentatively handled due to various censorship concerns around race and age, but Jo's hesitancy is also faithful to the character. She is anxiously ambivalent about sexual pleasure, demonstrated by an awkward mid-embrace exchange: 'don't do that', 'why not?', 'I like it'. But finally her wish for a moment of closeness and happiness wins out, even if it proves transitory: 'I'll probably never see you again, I know it … But I don't care. Stay with me now, it's enough.' The film's pressbook describes it as 'Jo's form of protest, her way of saying to hell with tomorrow if today is fun'.[112]

The morning after, Jo's last sight of Jimmy comes as she watches his ship sail away, Jimmy sitting on deck peeling potatoes, oblivious to Jo's fond observation from afar. The soft samba-tinged variation of the score's main theme plays over this lengthy farewell, marking the poignant finality of the moment. Finally, the ever more tiny and distant figure disappears inside: Jo has taken love's last look. She will later transform him into a figure of myth, 'son of a chieftain', Prince Ossini 'from darkest Africa', with skin as black as coal who could sing and dance, the very stuff of orientalist myth that Jimmy and Jo had previously made fun of, and a completely inaccurate version of her Liverpudlian lover. An interesting point: in the original play, Jimmy had been from Cardiff and the change to Liverpool, intentionally or not, connects him to the phenomenon of the 'Cunard Yanks', Liverpool seamen who worked the big transatlantic ships, bringing tastes of exotic US culture back home, including novelties and toys (like Jimmy's smart little wind-up car), new fashions, and perhaps most influentially of all new records and guitars (Liverpool's Cunard Yanks were instrumental to the musical culture that nurtured The Beatles). Men from big ships bring exciting, potentially life-altering cargo when they dock; they forge new cultural connections. Jimmy sparks Jo's romantic aspirations and imaginings but she'll be left pregnant as a result: as Geoff later observes, 'the dream's gone but the baby's real enough'.

3 'This is the place': An Interlude on Location, Landscape and Local Knowledge

At this point I wish to momentarily step back from the film's narrative flow and take some time to explore different critical attitudes to its evocation of place, arguably one of its most commented on and contentious elements, as with other films of the British New Wave. Although generally warmly received by many critics, in some quarters (like the hostile publication *Movie*) the New Wave films were accused of gratuitous 'landscape-monger[ing]' and recourse to Northern cliché to the point where, Thomas Elsaesser suggested, 'the scene of a couple overlooking belching gas-works and a row of sooty houses from the surrounding hills became as meaningful as a shot of the Eiffel tower in a picture about Paris.'[113] In work that has proven highly influential in subsequent scholarship, both Andrew Higson and John Hill went on to identify significant problems with the New Wave's presentation of landscapes, which for them functioned not so much as settings but exoticised spectacles encouraging 'a form of cultural tourism'.[114] For Hill, 'place rather than action' predominated in the New Wave, with excessive aestheticised location shots that 'only loosely fit into the logic of narrative development'.[115] Higson identified 'That Long Shot of Our Town from That Hill' (the phrase was originally director John Krish's) as the New Wave's totemic image, arguing that it represented an 'external point of view from outside and above the city, the look of the master-cameraman, the sympathetic gaze of the bourgeoisie'.[116] The middle-class provenance of most of the movement's directors only underlined the 'position of visual mastery' and 'class authority' represented by these shots: 'the voyeurism of one class looking at another'.[117] This visual language fatally undermined any idea that these films might be showing working-class life from the inside.

Higson's and Hill's critiques have become firmly established within the scholarly historiography of British cinema, but not without challenge. Peter Hutchings suggested that some of the landscape location shots that they invested with particular ideological meanings might equally be 'explicable within the established conventions of the establishing shot', while B. F. Taylor argues that the movement was judged by narrow and overdetermined criteria, with 'the use of locations in other modes of cinema rarely questioned and/or criticised to the same extent as it has been in relation to the British New Wave'.[118] The emphasis on this single aspect of the films, to the near exclusion of anything else, has resulted in a critical approach as weirdly skewed, Taylor suggests, as reading classical Hollywood Westerns solely in terms of how they 'use prairie landscapes to help over-contextualise their narratives and overemphasise their settings'.[119]

Both Hill and Higson analysed sequences from *A Taste of Honey* to support their argumentation. Hill reads Jo's long walk home from school along the ship canal in terms of excess 'landscape-mongering', with 'a series of seven shots (lasting nearly fifty seconds) before the sequence is infused with a narrative significance by the appearance of Jimmy'.[120] But there are other ways of reading this sequence, B. F. Taylor counters: that actually it 'does fit neatly into the film's narrative unfolding. Jo is taking her time getting home because she is waiting for Helen and her lover to be out. Also, as we soon learn, Jo often

Jo as *flâneuse*, her aesthetic wanderings rendered through slow dissolves

walks this way home.'[121] I would go even further and suggest that this scene is vital to the characterisation of Jo as a kind of aesthete, here an urban *flâneuse*, pleasurably meandering home while taking in her surroundings, as Delaney suggests in her screenplay direction: 'She wanders aimlessly along the canal bank … deserted and desolate. JO is quite happy.'[122] The long dissolves also add to the mood of aesthetic contemplation. From the outset, we are shown how Jo is sharply attuned to the look of things around her: the very first thing she does when she and Helen enter their new rented room is to stand on a chair to tie a silk scarf around the bare light bulb to diffuse its harsh glare and create a more aesthetically pleasing environment. We also see how Jo transfigures the stuff of her everyday life into art through that spilled portfolio of sketches. And without wanting to simplistically over-equate Shelagh Delaney with her character, the writer lyricised the beauty of the industrial landscape of her native Salford in her 1960 *Monitor* documentary, describing it as 'restless with all the coming and the going', warm and alive, 'a dirty place too I suppose, but at the same time it's dramatic … even romantic if you can stand the smell', exerting a pull on her 'like a terrible drug'. Therefore, why wouldn't an aesthetically inclined young woman like Jo choose to linger on the quayside and take in the sights, the wide canal bisecting the city with its intricate system of bridges, locks and basins, and the impressive bulk of the big ships from all over the world, conjuring her own aestheticised experience of her restless, romantic hometown? The insistence on seeing aestheticisation as inevitably an external viewpoint, as in Higson's suggestion that 'it is only from a class position outside the city that the city can appear beautiful', seems quite limited and denies the possibility that working-class protagonists may occupy the subject position of aesthete themselves.[123]

This possibility is partially acknowledged in Higson's commentary on the only pure example of 'That Long Shot of Our Town from That Hill' in *A Taste of Honey*, which occurs as Jo looks out of the kitchenette window of her attic flat onto a typical 'undifferentiated mass of houses, factories, chimneys and so forth

falling away from the point of vision'.[124] Higson reads Jo in this
moment as 'imprisoned within the city but desiring to get outside
it ... fixed behind the bars of the window looking out from an
"imaginary" vantage point, the figure of what might be, if only ...'[125]
But as with her canal-side wanderings, there are other ways we might
read this moment. Pragmatically, it is Jo contemplating an enforced
early morning start (which is why the streets below are empty) and
surveying the distance she has to travel to get to school now that
they have moved to the other side of town (she says as much to her
mother later). Rather than being a 'gratuitous spectacle', the shot
of the city rooftops partly functions as an establishing shot for a
longer sequence.[126] I would query the suggestion that its 'occupation
of screen time seems inordinately long' (it lasts only a few seconds),
but its slow pace does seem to usher in a more contemplative
feel, suggestive perhaps of the reluctance to hurry out on a cold
morning.[127] The succeeding interior shot's combination of subdued
natural lighting (pale sunlight filtered by net curtains) and the rough
granularity of the film stock, with sensitive dressing of the space
(those old-fashioned earthenware hot water bottles stashed on a low
shelf suggesting the tactics needed to combat the cold, contrasting
with the steamy warmth emanating from the kettle on the hob), and

the positioning of Jo to the side of the frame, leaning against the wall, hands clasped around her teacup, are reminiscent of Vermeer's depictions of young women in everyday domesticity. It is a moment of quiet 'undramatic achievement', mundane but poetic, as Andrew Klevan describes similar scenes in films by Ozu and Bresson (even though a film like *A Taste of Honey* would never usually be placed in such company).[128] To me, it feels less like an externally imposed aestheticisation of imprisoning squalor (that criticism of bourgeois voyeurism that always stalks the British New Wave), than a scene of haptic sensuality, conveying Jo's experience of pausing and quietly drinking hot tea before going out on a cold early morning. Its transcendence comes from its quotidian groundedness rather than any aspiration towards social elevation or escape.

Dave Forrest's intervention in the debates about classed aesthetics and British screen realism is relevant here, particularly the way he places the work of contemporary working-class director Shane Meadows in dialogue with the British New Wave. While acknowledging Hill's and Higson's 'understandable uneasiness with the connotations of a middle-class approach to a working-class subject', he asks what happens when those same visual tropes occur in the oeuvre of a working-class film-maker:

When Meadows places one of his young protagonists against a vast expanse,
emphasizing alienation from his or her environment, are we to think, as
Higson does in relation to similar motifs in the New Wave, that the director is
engaging in 'cultural tourism'?[129]

For Forrest, the existence of these 'shared qualities' across films of
very different class provenance only serves to 'reveal the limitations
of basing an understanding of the films' aesthetic construction
on a sociohistorical platform'.[130] In terms of optical politics and
social reality, the straightforward equation of an elevated view with
bourgeois mastery seems unsustainable.[131] Going up a hill, for the
purposes of exercise, or solitude, or courtship, or just to enjoy the
view, is embedded in working-class life, evident even in the play of
A Taste of Honey, which includes Helen's childhood recollections:
'I used to climb up there every day and sit on the top of the hill, and
you could see the mills in the distance.'[132] It figures in the nursery
rhyme Jo and Geoff recite repeatedly, 'Pippin Hill', and in the song
sung in a round by the canal, 'On a hill there is a lady'. In the Peak
District specifically (where Jo and Geoff go on a spontaneous daytrip),
Stuart Maconie notes the 'long tradition of factory workers hiking
out there on their Sundays off', including the mass trespass on Kinder
Scout in the 1930s that established the right to roam.[133] Viewing Our
Town from That Hill didn't have to mean insinuating oneself into the
employer's viewpoint; it could be an act of radical reclamation.

The Higson/Hill paradigm prioritises the agency of directors,
usually middle-class, over the authors who originated the narratives
and often adapted them for the screen, who were frequently of
working-class background and did know the places and communities
being represented. Indeed Terry Lovell's suggestion that the New
Wave's viewpoint was closer to the class position of Hoggart's
'scholarship boy' ('someone deeply implicated in and familiar with
what is observed: someone who has left that life behind, yet with a
considerable sense of loss in moving through the educational system,
and who therefore brings to its observation the knowledge of the

insider combined with the distance achieved by the move outside and beyond') sounds closest to the class journey taken by the cohort of working-class writers who contributed to the British New Wave, including Delaney.[134] But the presumed supremacy of the director in setting the visual tone has obscured how important the input of the 'native' writer could be to the British New Wave, especially so with a writer like Delaney, already assumed by dint of age and gender to be a lesser contributor. *A Taste of Honey*, as Lavinia Brydon argues, 'originates and develops from personal observations about *her* home city', she was the person who had the deepest knowledge of the area being filmed, and her script, steeped in intimate local knowledge, provided 'a template from which Richardson and Lassally clearly worked'.[135] Delaney's script notes for the crosstown bus journey that begins *A Taste of Honey* bear obvious traces of specific local knowledge as well as providing guidance for the overall visual tone:

We see the centre of Manchester, Piccadilly – a very crowded place with plenty of lights and plenty going on. Then as the bus leaves the city centre behind everything is much quieter as it travels down through Chapel Street, Salford – past Salford Royal Hospital and the River Irwell – seeing silent housetops and church spires and chimneys, and great black granite monuments and statues erected to great men of the past – Oliver Cromwell, Robert Peel.[136]

Stephen Frears attested to Delaney's 'eye for the best shot, the right location, the perspective' when they were making the later Salford-set film *Charlie Bubbles*, and there is no reason to doubt that she had a similar eye when working on *A Taste of Honey*, which therefore makes it 'especially troubling', as Brydon suggests, to see 'her contribution to the film's atmospheric sense of place' effaced.[137]

Although Terry Lovell's account of *A Taste of Honey* had tried to bring Shelagh Delaney back into the discussion, it did this by separating Delaney's original concept from what she saw as Tony Richardson's Hoggartian additions, arguing that 'Delaney's play did not inhabit the structure of feeling articulated by *The Uses of Literacy* but was sutured onto it in the film adaptation' and therefore:

Hill's and Higson's analyses work best on those parts of *A Taste of Honey* which were introduced in the film and have no counterpart in Delaney's play – the location sequences in and around Manchester, and the visit to Blackpool. In these sequences we find the familiar concern with the quality of new working-class culture, expressed within the visual terms and references common to the New Wave.[138]

In similar vein, Selina Todd has more recently opined that Richardson superimposed a 'supposedly traditional working-class culture of nursery rhymes, untamed moorland and fairs' onto Delaney's original, removing any sense of contemporaneity and instead 'present[ing] working-class life as a timeless cycle of seasonal festivals'.[139] However, access to Delaney's screenplay drafts for *A Taste of Honey* makes clear how many of the elements Lovell and Todd attribute retrospectively to Richardson actually derive from the original author herself, as she adapted and expanded her own play. For instance, the Blackpool sequences that are read as the imposition of Hoggartian puritanism about brash popular culture (as well as a Free Cinema borrowing from Lindsay Anderson's sour 1953 docu-diatribe *O Dreamland*) can in fact be traced back in conception to Delaney's initial screenplay: 'The impression must be here of a nightmarish and monstrous funfair, seen entirely through JO's eyes. Everything is shot so that the most mechanical, enormous and vulgar aspect of the place is emphasised.'[140] Likewise, the Whit Week Walks sequence that both Hill and Lovell identify as Richardson's directorial embellishment actually comes directly from Delaney. Rather than having this kind of scene-setting local colour foisted upon her reluctantly, she originated it herself and was keen to include more of it, writing an additional (unused) May Day ritual into her first draft screenplay, which she explained to the reader in quasi-anthropological detail:

In the North of England at any rate it is customary for all children under fourteen to dress up in various outlandish costumes – any old rags and tat they can find – soot on their faces – old bowler hats on their heads, etc. and go round the streets with a collecting box – usually an old cocoa tin on a piece of string, nosing on people's front doors and singing:

> We come to greet you all this day
> And hope you will not turn us away
> For we laugh and we sing
> In a merry ring
> On the first of May.[141]

V. F. Perkins had asserted that 'Richardson tarts up *A Taste of Honey* with his street games' but their true provenance was Delaney.[142] Her original play had Helen recalling seasonal childhood rituals ('in the summer we had singing games and in the spring we played with tops and hoops, and then in the autumn there was the Fifth of November, then we used to have bonfires in the street, and gingerbread and all that'), which are then extrapolated in the film, particularly in the recurrent presence of children on the streets, playing, singing, rhyming and chanting, echoed in the film's score.[143] The publication in 1959 of Iona and Peter Opie's anthropological work *The Lore and Language of Schoolchildren* had heightened interest in this fascinating and surprisingly robust oral tradition and may well have inspired Delaney to expand upon this aspect of her play when adapting it for the screen.[144] But her interest was far from ephemeral: phrases from children's rhymes and songs provided titles for several of her works in the ensuing decades, such as her 2004 BBC radio drama *Baloney Said Salome*. The presence of children playing in the street as part of the Salford cityscape was primarily born of Delaney's personal knowledge. In her *Monitor* documentary, she emphasised their ubiquity: 'This place is alive with kids, they're all over the place wherever you go, sucking toffees and chewing gum and eating ice cream and chocolate and teeming like ants everywhere.'

'This place is alive with kids'

Some critics may have regarded the swarming children in the film as a bit contrived (or '*voulu*', as the poet Philip Larkin put it in a letter, although he otherwise enjoyed the film), but they were nonetheless grounded in Delaney's own observations and memories.[145]

It is very clear that Shelagh Delaney was deeply, passionately engaged with matters of place, space, location and the local. Even the first words of her first play were the spatially orientated statement 'This is the place'. The feted young writer still lived in Salford but extended stays in London and international travel had granted her new comparative perspectives on what was distinctive about her hometown.[146] She reflects on this in the *Monitor* documentary, which was timed to coincide with her second, much more community-focused ensemble piece, *The Lion in Love*, but also provides an insight into her mindset around the time she was working on the *Taste of Honey* screenplay. She characterises Salford and its people as literally grounded in their location: 'the language is alive … and you know exactly where it's coming from, right out of the earth', in a close community that 'seems to generate a terrific warmth. Down here you can almost hear the heart of the city beating.' Delaney explored the ambivalent pull of the place as somewhere 'you want to get away from' even while it was 'worth its weight in gold' to a writer. It was 'secure as anything', like a rock, but at the same time 'old and crumbling and neglected' and seemed almost 'to be dying'. She was especially perturbed by the drastic urban redevelopment gathering pace at that time in Salford, as well as many other British towns and cities, which saw dilapidated housing designated slum dwellings demolished in record numbers, 'as their intimate, intensely human world disappeared forever', in the words of historian David Kynaston.[147] A reporter visiting Salford in 1959 noted how 'people whose roots are firmly embedded in the hard ground show every sign that they are not going to take kindly to the sudden upheaval', and Delaney certainly didn't, publicly expressing her disquiet at the council 'tearing down whole parts of Salford' and sending people 'away, far away' to remote estates, 'sterile places' where 'there's no neighbourliness, it takes years to do this'.[148]

Salford led the way in the construction of multistorey housing to replace its demolished terraces and in 1959 plans to construct a number of fifteen-storey tower blocks were announced (the growth of this elevated model for working-class housing would further disrupt any easy identification between height and social power, with a view from a high window soon signifying poverty and isolation rather than 'visual mastery'). And it was to this image of the tower block that Delaney turned thirty years later, when she had been asked to write a sequel explaining what happened next to the characters of *A Taste of Honey*.[149] She focused on how they'd been impacted by councils in the grip of 'a massive rush of civic pride to their heads' who embarked on 'frenzied and irrational' community redevelopment.[150] Hence Helen, Jo and Jo's baby son find themselves forcibly reallocated into a new twelfth-floor flat, which drives Helen to fatal despair:

Helen stood on the small, square, bleak balcony attached to the outside of the flat like a feeding dish to the bars of a pet budgerigar's cage. She looked at what the Town Hall's publicity machine described as breathtaking views of Manchester. The wind howled. Her eyes watered. She decided to die.[151]

Delaney tells us that after Helen's self-willed death, Jo became an artist and moved abroad but 'the image of her mother standing on the small, square, stone balcony and deciding to die is still vivid. She still paints it, one way and another, after so many years.'[152] While this later material may not be 'canon', it provides some fascinating insights into exactly how definingly important these battles over the landscape of Salford were to Delaney. No sentimentalist, Delaney was fully aware of the dangers of exoticising urban desolation but at the same time was very alive to the brick terrace's grim beauty and unique warmth. Her 'conflicted stance' over the aestheticisation of slums, Lavinia Brydon suggests, is encapsulated in *Charlie Bubbles*, as glum Mancunian Charlie and his enthusiastic American PA Eliza form very different opinions of the rubbish-strewn wastelands of his semi-derelict former neighbourhood.[153] Delaney was attuned to the human costs of indiscriminate redevelopment (or worse still, the deliberate decimation of cohesive working-class communities in order to better control and discipline them). It is interesting that she turned down Tony Warren's invitation to write for *Coronation Street* because she feared it played into nostalgic stereotypes of Northern communities as 'cap and muffler' territory.[154] But at the same time, she had a strong preservationist instinct towards her hometown, its customs, its communities and its topographic specificities (including buildings being torn down at an alarming rate) both in her activism and in her creative work. Film could play a particularly powerful role in this, recording places and celebrating them before they were flattened by the wrecking ball.

Most previous scholarship on the British New Wave and on *A Taste of Honey* has inadequately acknowledged how an author like Delaney, so passionately engaged with place, location and landscape, might play a crucial role in the film's approach to it. An intense interest in these areas wasn't something bolted onto the film by an aestheticising director and cinematographer, but was emphatically the product of a collaborative enterprise, bringing together intimate local knowledge and technical originality to co-create a vision of Salford that was both lyrical *and* authentic.

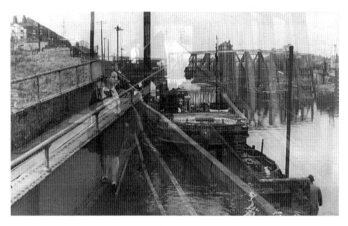

4 Unique, Young, Unrivalled, Smashing: Jo's Progress

While the first part of *A Taste of Honey* belongs to Jo and Jimmy's romance, the second half centres on its consequences in the shape of Jo's pregnancy as well as her close friendship with Geoff. They first meet in the shoe shop where Jo works, when she sells him a pair of fashionable 'Italian casuals' in the sale, before meeting again by chance at the Whit Week parade. And if Jimmy had proved a potentially controversial character, then Geoff would bring into play another set of controversies, attracting considerable attention from the BBFC, just as the play before it had ignited intense discussion

A reverse Cinderella 'meet cute': Jo offers the shoe to Geoff

around representing homosexuality (dramatic territory that until 1957 had been completely vetoed by the Lord Chamberlain's Office). Under John Trevelyan's leadership, the BBFC was undergoing a parallel process of liberalisation and in May 1960, just as two Oscar Wilde biopics went on release, they received pre-production documentation for a further two film projects dealing with homosexual themes in contemporary rather than historical settings, *A Taste of Honey* and *Victim* (1961). But whereas the latter was a social problem film entirely concerned with homosexuality as its main theme, featuring a coruscating central performance from Dirk Bogarde as a closeted blackmailed lawyer, in *A Taste of Honey* Murray Melvin's Geoff happens to be gay but this is only one of several narrative threads woven through the film. Both films trade on a fascination with the hidden (to many) cultures of homosexuality, *Victim* through its deployment of a police investigation narrative to allow unusually unfettered access to gay subcultures, and *A Taste of Honey* through Jo's questioning of Geoff about his sexuality, acting as a proxy for (some of) the audience: 'I've always wanted to know about people like you ... I want to know what you do. I want to know why you do it.' 'I don't go in for sensational confessions' is his comeback, contrasting to *Victim*, which centres precisely on a 'sensational confession': Bogarde's character admitting to his wife that he sexually desired a man ('I wanted him!'), which Andy Medhurst rightly identifies as a huge moment, directly voicing gay male desire for the first time in mainstream British cinema.[155]

A Taste of Honey downplays any suggestion of equivalent forceful desire on Geoff's part, except in the oblique allusion to his former landlady's reason for evicting him (catching him with a man). Instead queer identity is signified through representational tropes, some of which perhaps verge on the stereotypical: his natty 'proto-mod' zip-up jacket and jeans, which could come straight from the Vince Man's Shop catalogue, and his espadrille-esque continental shoes, his training to be a textile designer, and his facility with domestic duties like cooking, cleaning and sewing.[156] On one hand,

Geoff's complete devotion to Jo ('being with you's me life') could be seen as problematic in his sacrifice of his own wishes in service of hers ('you've got to have someone to love you while you're looking for someone to love'), a formative example of what would become the representational cliché of a gay man as best friend to a straight heroine, helpmeet to heterosexuality but disconnected from any sense of gay communality; indeed Robin Griffiths argues that Geoff's 'emergent and groundbreaking cinematic visibility' is counterbalanced by 'the unthreatening asexuality that the film actually presents'.[157] But on the other hand, the very unsensationalism of Geoff, and the refusal of the film to place him forcibly at the centre of torrid melodrama but instead to present him as queer *and* quotidian, has its own progressive potential in an era when homosexual relations were still illegal. Dirk Bogarde certainly thought so, according to Murray Melvin, who recalled Bogarde telling him when they were making *HMS Defiant* (1962) together that he thought Melvin's portrayal of Geoff had done more representational good in ten minutes than he felt he had achieved in the whole of *Victim*.[158] While Tony Richardson never publicly acknowledged his own bisexuality, his 'intuitive sympathy for the social outsider', along with his casting of Paul Danquah and Murray Melvin in key roles – later to turn up as a trendy couple visiting Rita Tushingham's boutique in *Smashing Time* (1967) – and all the characters' refusal to stay safely within the parameters of heteronormative respectability (even Peter gooses Geoff and tells him 'don't worry, I know the district', implying his own possible bisexuality), undeniably imbued *A Taste of Honey* with a queer sensibility.[159]

Geoff may be an archetypal 'sad young man' of the kind identified by Richard Dyer as central to gay typology, performed with downcast eyes and demure posture by Melvin, but along with his empathetic melancholy, he has a nice line in droll humour (the scene when Jo is moaning about her various ailments while Geoff gives her short shrift is a fantastic comic vignette: 'I've got toothache', 'yes, I've got bloody heartache').[160] He is a 'funny man', to use Jo's words, in

Never all together in the film itself, Melvin, Tushingham and Danquah meet up during location shooting

both its senses within British vernacular, constructed as 'funny peculiar' (or 'queer', another word with dual meaning) by dint of his sexuality but also 'funny ha ha', humorous and playful, and therefore recalling Jo's earlier relationship with Jimmy. Geoff is, in Jo's words again, 'unique', and defies any easy stereotyping. Melvin recalled pushing back against the suggestion he should adopt a 'mincing' walk that would be imitated by the neighbourhood children, precisely to avoid glib stereotypical humour at the expense of his character's dignity.[161]

Both Geoff and Jo are simultaneously ordinary and extraordinary, as Jo sets out in her rallying speech under the arches when she is worried about her pregnancy and feeling at a low ebb and Geoff reassures her that she'll soon be back to her 'usual self'. Climbing to the top of the hill, she turns back and asks, 'And what is my usual self? My usual self is a very unusual self and don't you

forget it, Geoffrey Ingham. I'm an extraordinary person!', elongating
the vowel sounds and extending her arms into the air, defiantly
taking up space and making noise despite her humbling predicament.
'There's only one of me, like there's only one of you,' she continues,
pointing to herself and then to Geoff, inviting him into her bubble of
personal pride. What's really striking here is the sudden uplift from
the dire straits of Jo's situation, pregnant and unmarried – the grim
material of social realism – into a sudden outburst of self-confidence

and exuberance that dares to appropriate the outrageous hyperbole of film trailers and let these friends apply it to themselves. 'We're unique', 'young', 'unrivalled', 'smashing', 'we're bloody marvellous', they tell each other, echoing beneath and then running out from under the viaduct, the Victorian industrial infrastructure that defines and dominates their world, into the sunlight, Geoff even taking flight with a little jump at the top of the slope (That Shot of His Jump on That Hill?). Lassally's camerawork incorporates the changeability of the weather beautifully here, with the emotional shift coinciding with a sudden serendipitous break in the clouds. It's a moment that seems to push onwards into the optimism of the 1960s and a new emphasis on youth, social mobility and possibility. It also provides a powerful expression of the bond shared by Jo and Geoff, fellow misfits who have every reason to be permanently downcast but refuse to be, and who have found each other. It is one of the most resonant moments in postwar British culture, a clarion call to outsiders everywhere to embrace their alterity and join forces with those who feel the same.

Comrades in being 'bloody marvellous', Jo and Geoff build a home together that expresses their utopian aspirations. Motivated by her deeply held desire for a place of her own, Jo uses her first pay packet to rent a large open-plan flat. Despite rejecting art college,

Jo ends up living somewhere strongly reminiscent of an artist's studio in repurposed industrial space. Furnished with only the barest essentials when Geoff moves in, he brings his creative flair and practical capability to bear on the place and together they set about transforming it into a homely but bohemian nest. A charming makeover montage ensues, fit to keep company with the cabin transformation in *Calamity Jane* (1953) as an iconic queer-inflected home-making scene, and faithful throughout to Delaney's instruction that its 'emphasis will be on the domestic and the ordinary' and 'the impression will be of their growing relationship'.[162] We see Jo and Geoff cleaning the windowpanes inside and out, shaking out dusty rugs and hanging up brightly patterned modern curtains, with Geoff fixing a Chinese paper lantern over the bare light bulb (and we already know what an important marker of homeliness that is for Jo) and chalking a ballet mural onto one of the bare walls. Later he will draw Jo in the guise of 1920s flapper and tack that sketch to the wall too, joining their art postcards and travel posters for the Côte d'Azur, Pietrasanta and the Pyrenees, speaking to their aspirations towards European cosmopolitanism, just like Geoff's Italian-style shoes or his purchase of garlic and spaghetti (a detail that didn't make it into the final film but is there in the draft screenplay). To complete the picture of domestic bliss, a white cat nurses her kittens by the stove in an upturned box labelled 'the house of quality', a slogan equally applicable to the home Jo and Geoff have co-created.

Domestic bliss in 'the house of quality'

Their ramshackle but charmingly arty flat contrasts totally with the bay-windowed bungalow that Helen has now found herself living in with Peter. The interior's contemporary trappings are alternately flouncy fussy and spiky spindly, from its swagged net curtains to the picador-style spears in the cocktail cabinet, while Helen's narcissistic tendencies are suggested by her own framed picture sitting on the mantelpiece. Everything looks a bit insubstantial and gimcrack. The complex expressive detail in the *mise en scène* in these opposing homes is partly attributable to art director Ralph Brinton and his assistant Ted Marshall, dressing interior spaces with the same skill and care they brought to scouting exterior locations. Although domestic interiors have tended to receive much less critical attention in scholarship on the British New Wave, they are as important to the films as the wider landscapes. In *A Taste of Honey*, Jo's shifting emotions and allegiances are reflected in the different rooms she inhabits (which are further differentiated by being shot with film stocks of varying granularity), and imagery associated with indoor domestic spaces was also crucial to the film's marketing, with worn, patched wallpaper providing the basis for the design for its main UK poster, not a location shot of a cobbled street.

Although Selina Todd reads Jo and Geoff's shared flat as the imposition upon Delaney's play of 'Hoggart's "cosy burrow", removed from the linear passage of time in the harsh outside world', thereby depoliticising her work, I see their creation of a home in the film as profoundly political.[163] It is not merely a safe retreat from the world for two fey 'babes-in-the-wood' but the proving ground for an alternative model of family that departs from prevailing conventions. It may not be 'marrying love' between Jo and Geoff, as she points out, but they go about setting up a family unit regardless, with Geoff alternately acting as friend, partner and 'big sister' to Jo. Moreover, their home is not presented as separate from the wider community but embedded within it, as their friendly familiarity with the neighbourhood children proves. Their difference has not resulted in pariahdom, even when Jo dares to liken their set-up to communism, playing on cold war paranoia to provoke her mother when she visits (for all that Todd suggests the film disconnects Delaney's story from contemporary concerns and places it in 'a vaguely post-war present', this kind of detail, just like the prominent CND badge on Jo's lapel, helps to situate the story in a definite milieu[164]).

'We're communists too': Jo tries a bit of political provocation

But Jo and Geoff's alliance is not without its conflicts and ambivalences, as Geoff is wary but nonetheless keen to care for Jo and act as prospective father to her baby, while Jo struggles with feeling 'stifled', irritated at her own dependency, trying to assert 'I'm everything to myself.' Pregnancy and impending motherhood provide Jo with chastening lessons in vulnerability, and she voices her rejection of all that it entails both ideologically and physically ('Fourth month: constipation' and the prospect of 'cannibalistic' breastfeeding), baldly stating, 'I hate motherhood.' She may be momentarily surprised and delighted by feeling her baby kick inside her for the first time – and Rita Tushingham acts this moment beautifully, Jo's face suddenly lighting up at the dawning realisation of what's happened – but this takes place in an ultra-precarious situation (on a makeshift raft floating on the canal as a thunderstorm approaches) and it doesn't magically erase deeply felt animosities

Anticipating motherhood: ecstasy and agony

and fears. When Geoff brings an educational doll back from the
clinic to help Jo practise infant care before her baby arrives, she gives
voice to her anger in the gothic environs of the churchyard: 'I'll bash
its brains out, I'll kill it. I don't want this baby, Geoff, I don't want
to be a mother! I don't want to be a woman!' – especially shocking
statements in an era when motherhood was very much revered.

Jo's pregnancy is shadowed by numerous interlocking anxieties:
about raising her child alone without an income, about the social
stigma of her baby not being white, and about being a carrier for
hereditary madness or intellectual disability. Helen's story of Jo's
Irish father being 'a bit simple' ('everybody used to laugh at him but I
thought he was rather nice') and Jo having inherited his 'funny eyes'
prompts Jo to worry about what it means for her unborn child that
her own father 'lived in a twilight world ... the land of the daft'. As
Jo expresses fears that her baby 'will be born dead or daft', the word
takes on a weightier meaning than it previously had in her light banter
with Jimmy. The teeming children playing in the dirt by the canal or in
the graveyard become outward manifestations of Jo's inner worries.
She's barely beyond a damaged childhood herself and clearly anxious
about repeating the same pattern of neglect, abjecting those fears onto
other mothers: 'think of the harm she does having children'.[165] Like
the children singing in a round, making interlocking, repeating sonic
patterns that seem more automatic than volitional, Jo finds herself
pitched into playing her part in the ongoing eternal cycle of life and
death. The sight of a dead bird on the cold, wet gravestones in the
churchyard prompts her to express her mortal thoughts: 'A bit of
love, a bit of lust, and there you are. We don't ask for life, we have it
thrust upon us.' Deeper timescales than a single linear life seem to be
evoked in this moment, linking sex and maternity to a sense of endless
repetition stretching into infinity (forging interesting connections, as
Terry Lovell suggested, to Julia Kristeva's notion of 'woman's time' as
non-linear and cyclical).[166] The geological accretion of the stalactites
slowly forming in the deep underground cavern Jo and Geoff visit on
their day out suggests this much bigger temporal scale, as do the folk

Deep time: Jo and Geoff among the stalactites

rituals that punctuate the story whose origins are lost in antiquity. Against such temporalities, the individual, however 'extraordinary', is rendered minuscule and meaningless.

Throughout this fraught anticipation, Geoff continues to support and care for Jo, consolidating their improvised queer family. When tensions and other unfulfilled yearnings rise to the surface, they can be allayed with rueful realism about life's inevitable disappointments: 'Who's happy?' Geoff asks. Or a little bit of fey escapism might provide a distraction, like reciting the nursery rhyme 'Pippin Hill' together (reminiscent of the use of the childlike bears and squirrels roleplay as safe common ground in *Look Back in Anger*). There are pleasures in domesticity too, as Geoff bakes a cherry cake in a shiny silver cake tin (shown to best advantage through Lassally's use of fine-grained film here) and brings it to the table held 'high above his head like the crown jewels or something', Delaney suggested in her

A ceremonial cherry cake 'like the crown jewels'

screenplay, while humming the wedding march, placing it on a table set with a crisp white cloth and chic Midwinter-style tableware.[167] The baby is expected soon, and there may be a sly reference to Peter's slang comment on Jo's 'bun in the oven' in this little homely ceremony. But their domestic utopia is about to be interrupted by the reappearance of Helen, arriving on bonfire night to set off a few fireworks of her own.

A passive-aggressive battle for supremacy ensues between Geoff and Helen, in which Geoff seems hopelessly outflanked. The cold set of Helen's eyes descends as she takes off her hat, making clear her intention to stay, while a cowed Geoff picks up his bag indicating that he will go, despite Jo's stated wishes: 'Helen, I want Geoffrey to stay, understand?' Instead she picks up the broom as though to sweep him out of the door. In Delaney's first draft script, Helen was even more direct: 'Two's company. Sling your hook.'[168] Most cruelly of all, she orders him to take away the Moses basket he and Jo chose together, to be usurped by the new cot she's purchased. Geoff departs with downcast gaze and an empty cradle by his side, the epitome of the 'sad young man', as the ballerinas in his mural behind him strike attitudes of lamentation. The cake that had been brought in with 'a quiet frenzy of high spirits' instead becomes the placeholder for Geoff's goodbye note, saying 'ta-ra' to Jo just as they had at their very first meeting in the shoe shop. Reading Geoff's strained attempt at a light tone leaves Jo in tears, frustrated and bereft at his departure and

how quickly he gave way to Helen: 'You clown, Geoff, you clown.' The radical potential represented by their queer family is thus all too prematurely curtailed.

* * *

Shelagh Delaney sometimes seemed to struggle to bring the dramas she wrote to a suitable close, epitomised by the ending of *Charlie Bubbles*, which has the hero simply rise above all his intractable woes in a conveniently placed but narratively inexplicable hot-air balloon.[169] The more grounded *A Taste of Honey* had the dramaturgic advantage of counting down to an imminent event: by the end of the narrative, Jo's pregnancy is full term and her baby due any time (and let's correct the canard Terry Lovell introduced that 'the film actually succeeds in giving Jo a ten-and-a-half month pregnancy, in spite of its much-proclaimed realism' – although in the play, Jo's baby is conceived at Christmas, there is no suggestion at all that the same timing applies in the film, making her labour pains manifesting in November perfectly acceptable in terms of gestational chronology).[170] Even building up to that non-negotiable endpoint, there was plenty of scope for variation and Delaney rewrote numerous versions of the concluding scenes of *A Taste of*

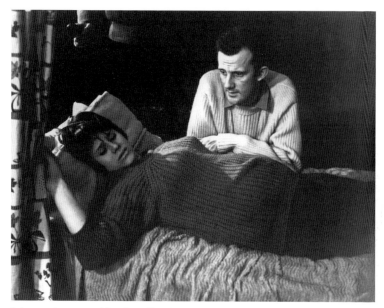

Labour pains: Tony Richardson directing Rita Tushingham

Honey, with considerable differences between each. Geoff was the
focus of Delaney's very first ending, left alone and suicidal after Helen
and a much kindlier Peter have whisked Jo away to live with them.
This changed at Theatre Workshop to Helen splitting up with Peter
and seeking out Jo but, shocked by Jo's statement that her baby 'may
be black', quickly leaving again to get a drink, possibly to return,
possibly not, as Jo waits and recites the 'Pippin Hill' nursery rhyme
all alone before the curtain falls. With the play's West End transfer,
more racist remarks were added to Helen's dialogue, which Stuart
Hall took issue with at the time, feeling them to be gratuitously
sensationalist and doing Helen's character 'a kind of violence which
she nowhere deserves'.[171] The Broadway production seems to have
toned down such potentially inflammatory elements and made Helen
more obviously empathetic, a tendency that arguably continued in
the film version. In Delaney's first draft screenplay, Helen's exit line

from the play about Jo's baby was retained but softened in its intent, as part of what Delaney called 'a moment of reconciliation and acceptance' between mother and daughter:

HELEN   We can always put him on the stage and call him 'Blackbird'. She puts her hand on JO's shoulder. JO smiles. There is a large sparkler in her hand, and her face is lit up by it.[172]

Jo's final words to Helen emphasised the mutuality of mother–daughter care: 'For the first time in my life I feel really important. I feel as if I could take care of everything. Even you.' This was still retained in the next version of the screenplay dated 3 March 1961, but with Jo now receiving a piece of treacle toffee from a young boy at the bonfire rather than having a sparkler. In the final version we see on screen, Delaney's original sparkler idea was revived but the explicit statement of daughterly care and confidence was left out and replaced with Helen's solicitous offer of a cup of tea when she gets back from the off-licence. Geoff observes from the shadows, almost returning to Jo when he thinks she's been abandoned but finally slipping away into the night once he sees Helen return. As Delaney's script put it: 'They are together now and there is no place for him.'[173] Such a remark would appear to endorse John Hill's suggestion that the film works to 'reaffirm the value of motherhood' and realign its wayward women 'back into a network of family relations', but as Robert Murphy suggests, 'Helen's cuckoo-like occupation of the nest which Jo and Geoffrey have built together hardly represents a reaffirmation of motherhood.'[174] Helen's mainly there because Peter's thrown her out in favour of a younger woman, and despite mother and daughter's temporary reconciliation, their everyday hostilities will no doubt be resumed. As he departs, Geoff seems melancholy but not emotionally devastated and is still able to take pleasure in the sight of the bonfire and the children's revels, although we might intuit certain ritualistic parallels between the Guy in flames atop the bonfire and the enforced ousting of Geoff, both sacrificial scapegoats.

Jo is not left alone to have her baby, as she is in the published playscript, but nonetheless a shot of her alone in her thoughts provides the final image of the film. A young boy lights Jo's sparkler with his own, passing on a spark from person to person, like the oral transmission of the songs and rhymes woven throughout the film. As it ignites, Jo holds it up, gazing impassively into its fizzling white heat. It still sparks away as the screen fades to black, concluding the film on an image of ongoing effervescence and expectancy that seems to relate to both mother and baby. It is a bittersweet moment combining loss with possibility, not just in terms of one individual but also a whole society undergoing profound change. And *A Taste of Honey*'s final shot is a close-up on a face. So much textual exegesis expounded on the film has focused on wide shots of landscapes. But if Tony Richardson's 'great gift' was, as one reviewer suggested, 'that he can show a face in close-up and reveal the thoughts of the mind without a word being spoken', then it seems important to pay attention to those intimate aspects of his film too.[175] *A Taste of Honey* is a film of faces as well as places, and as such its poetic final image of Jo's enigmatic look into her future provides a fitting conclusion.

5 Is There Honey Still for Tea?: Assessing the Film's Legacy

Woodfall's *A Taste of Honey* had its world premiere in London's Leicester Square on Thursday 14 September 1961. Exhibitors British Lion celebrated the event with 'a Lancashire hotpot party in a public house' nearby.[176] The gustatory theme, perhaps inevitable for a film with 'taste' in the title, continued into reviews that described it as 'satisfying as a good pint of beer' and its young star Rita Tushingham as 'a Lancashire hot-pot', a salty 'cup of winkles' and 'a garlic of a girl'.[177] Sometimes the appeal to taste was even more direct, as with a promotional tie-in stunt undertaken by a Birmingham cinema manager who 'had a bright idea to let his patrons know *A Taste of Honey* was on the way. For a week before playdate he offered them a taste of honey in the foyer! Both the honey and the biscuits on which it was served were promoted.'[178]

Critics and audiences alike found the film moreish. Reviewers relished its 'misty, moisty' poeticised scenography and, as Isabel Quigly suggested, it was 'hard to imagine if you'd never seen it on the stage how it was ever anything but a film'.[179] Much of the credit for this went to Woodfall, to Tony Richardson and to Walter Lassally, rather than to Shelagh Delaney. Meanwhile, Rita Tushingham was hailed as a major new star discovery, but the journalistic relish in specifying just how far she supposedly fell short from usual standards of screen pulchritude was highly revealing of the sexual politics and prejudices of the period, as this extended example from the *Daily Express* demonstrates:

She looks remarkably like Donald Duck's sister, always supposing he had one. The legs are so short that they seem to have been cut off just above the knees, and her backside waddles, when she walks – but not, repeat not, in the

An appeal to taste

manner of Miss Marilyn Monroe. The hair is mud-coloured, the face is like a relief map of Lancashire, and her name is, of all things, Rita Tushingham. Yet those who like them tall, those who like them blonde, those who like them stacked, those who like them slim, and those who like them elegant are nevertheless going to give their hearts to drab, dowdy, dumpy Miss Tushingham when they see her.[180]

At least Penelope Gilliatt's *Observer* review welcomed the young star for possessing 'the sort of face and quality that one has pined for through all the years of Surrey-rose ingenues'.[181] Dora Bryan and Murray Melvin were also singled out for extensive praise for their portrayals of Helen and Geoff, which would be reflected in their later award success.

Some still questioned *A Taste of Honey*'s realist credentials. When Tushingham remarked that she had been excited by the film's

British new waif: Rita Tushingham hits London

realist vision, rather than 'someone coming in and saying, "It's a lovely day, I've been picking roses in the garden"', a columnist in the *Daily Telegraph* sourly disagreed:

It depends what you mean by 'real'. It is quite possible that on an average lovely day in England there are more women picking roses in the garden than there are women living with homosexuals while they wait for their illegitimate half-caste babies to be born.[182]

But although its vision of contemporary verisimilitude may have been contentious in some quarters, it certainly didn't inhibit the film's box-office appeal. Despite not surpassing the extraordinary success of Woodfall's previous hit *Saturday Night and Sunday Morning*, Duncan Petrie notes that it was umbrella company Bryanston's 'biggest box office earner for 1961, netting a more modest but still significant profit of £29,064'.[183] *A Taste of Honey* was 'definitely a money-spinner', according to *Kine Weekly*'s end-of-year box-office round-up for 1961, going on to earn more into 1962.[184]

The film also went on to win multiple awards, including British Film Academy awards (forerunners of BAFTAs) for Best British Film, Best British Screenplay – with Delaney the first female winner in this category – as well as Best Actress (for Dora Bryan) and Most Promising Newcomer (for Rita Tushingham). And Shelagh Delaney and Tony Richardson were awarded the Best British Dramatic Screenplay of the year by The Writers' Guild of Great Britain. It enjoyed US success too, with a Golden Globe for Tushingham as Most Promising Female Newcomer, a Directors Guild nomination for Tony Richardson and a place in the National Board of Review's top ten best films.[185] There was further acclaim for the film on the Continent, with Best Actress and Actor awards at Cannes for Tushingham and Murray Melvin, as well as a Palme d'Or nomination, all lobbied for by François Truffaut, not usually a fan of British films: 'I saw *A Taste of Honey* at Cannes and I liked it a lot. It was at my insistence that the girl who plays the leading role got a prize.'[186] But so un-starry in appearance were Rita Tushingham and Dora Bryan that they were refused admittance to the Cannes gala reception at which they were due to be honoured, before critic Alexander Walker eventually spotted them outside and vouched for them to be let in.[187] Clearly, the traditional paradigms of stardom that Woodfall was trying to overturn had not shifted quite yet, but perhaps they had by the time Tushingham won another award at Cannes for the swinging London comedy *The Knack … and How to Get It* (1965), which also won the Palme d'Or. By then, the Oscars had already given their seal of approval for the new cinema emerging from Britain, as Woodfall's freewheeling period drama *Tom Jones* swept the board in 1964, giving Tony Richardson a career high of being designated Best Director of the Best Film that he never matched subsequently.

Delaney would continue to undertake insightful, subtle dramatic writing across multiple media in the decades to follow, a particular highlight being her screenplay for *Dance with a Stranger* (1985), but her career arguably never recovered from its meteoric origins, tending to overshadow everything that came after. *A Taste of Honey* was repeatedly revived over the years, and even received the dubious honour of making it onto the school curriculum. But Delaney was also kept in the public eye by the passionate fandom of Morrissey, singer and lyricist of key 1980s British band The Smiths, who 'never made any secret of the fact that at least 50 percent of my reason for writing can be blamed on Shelagh Delaney' and revelled in his fixation with his doughty, droll heroine.[188] Delaney's image adorned their record sleeves and textual borrowings from her work were sprinkled across numerous Smiths songs. For audiences of my generation, it is very difficult to disentangle *A Taste of Honey* from this powerful advocacy, which leads me to wonder whether the absolute centrality of Delaney to the mythology of Morrissey now presents a problem of reputational contamination. His public support for the far-right nationalist political party For Britain provided final irrefutable confirmation of his increasing rightward turn, with fans who had previously performed 'considerable mental gymnastics to absolve Morrissey' now 'out of plausible arguments'.[189] In spite of Morrissey reusing the line Delaney wrote for Jimmy in *A Taste of Honey* – 'dreamt of you last night, fell out of bed twice' – in his own lyrics, it seems that the nascent multiculturalism represented by the character, and by the child Jo is carrying, is being denied or refuted rather than accepted and embraced, and that is very sad.

This leads into bigger questions about the interpretation and deployment of historical cultural artefacts in service of what feels like an increasingly curdled national mythology. Owen Hatherley has written incisively of the sudden modern ubiquity of the 'Keep calm and carry on' wartime propaganda poster, the yearning for an imagined national identity of stoicism and tenacity it expressed quickly shading into 'narcissistic wallowing', while Sarah Manavis has noted new modes of racist repressive nostalgia operating in online local history groups using old photographs as evidence of a supposed prelapsarian past.[190] Old films are often put to work in this way too, as we can see in conservative commentator Simon Heffer's paean to the 'sanctuary' offered by British vintage film and television channel Talking Pictures TV whose content, in his view, 'celebrates the monoculture; it comes from an age when men were men and women were housewives, "diversity" was a word in hardly anyone's vocabulary', and portrays 'the England millions of us wish we still lived in':

It reminds us of an age when we were a steady, reliable, quietly heroic people who didn't engage in panic, self-hatred or self-congratulation. It is a land without face masks and hectoring, of live and let live and shrugging off with a bemused smile attempts to cause offence.[191]

Heffer presumptuously speaks for everyone who enjoys old films, pressing the films and their viewers alike into service as unwitting combatants in the contemporary culture wars where nostalgia is a key battleground.

In some respects, a film like *A Taste of Honey*, with its pub singalong, trip to the seaside and children playing out on the street at all hours, all eulogised as typical elements of 'the good old days' in countless sentimental memes, seems to invite a nostalgic gaze. Its capturing of real urban landscapes from the early 1960s, many of them since transformed or obliterated altogether, has the potential to work as a powerful mnemonic for times past and places gone. The film has also been a high-profile screening on Talking Pictures TV, the channel whose virtues Simon Heffer extols (while misunderstanding).[192] But at the same time, *A Taste of Honey* confounds any straightforward sense of cosiness in its vision of the past, showing the restricted horizons and ingrained prejudices that all the main characters have to contend with and chafe against. Practically all the elements of modern British society to which Heffer takes exception are present in the film: it is multicultural, not monocultural, it presents sexual diversity, its nurturing, empathetic male characters are Black or gay, and its heroines are not happily married housewives but sparky working-class lone mothers who answer back.[193] Its frank, funny, open-minded and forward-thinking ethos, combined with its sweetly lyrical approach to a situation that could otherwise be dismissed as squalid, provides the best possible refutation of any attempt to mobilise it in reactionary ways, and is what makes it a film of vital ongoing relevance.

Notes

1 Unsurprisingly, both the play and the film figure as a recurrent reference point across numerous histories of postwar Britain, from Kenneth O. Morgan, *The People's Peace: British History 1945–1990* (Oxford: Oxford University Press, 1990), pp. 142, 184–5, 200, to David Kynaston, *Modernity Britain, 1957–62* (London: Bloomsbury, 2015), pp. 147–8, 272–3, 705–6, to Arthur Marwick, *The Sixties* (Oxford: Oxford University Press, 1998), pp. 136–8.

2 I could write a whole additional book on the many interconnections between *A Taste of Honey* and The Beatles, from the iconographic similarities between the early presentation of the band and the film's aesthetics – when Ringo gets an afternoon off in *A Hard Day's Night* (1964), he wanders by a river among the scruffy kids playing there – to Geoff's line of dialogue 'your mother should know' allegedly inspiring Paul McCartney's composition of the same name. Selina Todd's biography of Shelagh Delaney suggests The Beatles admired her work and intriguingly mentions a later friendship with Ringo Starr. Selina Todd, *Tastes of Honey: The Making of Shelagh Delaney and a Cultural Revolution* (London: Chatto & Windus, 2019), p. 147.

3 Joan Littlewood, *Joan's Book* (London: Methuen, 2003), p. 517.

4 Eve Perrick, 'I still can't swallow this taste of honey', *Daily Mail*, 14 September 1961, p. 10.

5 Kenneth Tynan, 'At the theatre', *Observer*, 1 June 1958, p. 15.

6 'Editorial: The British Cinema', *Movie*, no. 1 (June 1962), p. 3.

7 'A Waste of Living', *Private Eye*, 1 June 1962, pp. 7–9.

8 Anthony Aldgate, *Censorship and the Permissive Society: British Cinema and Theatre 1955–1965* (Oxford: Clarendon Press, 1995), p. 122.

9 Richard Hoggart, *The Uses of Literacy* (Harmondsworth: Pelican, 1958), p. 46. As non-Hoggartian mams, Helen has a close contemporary in Elsie Tanner in *Coronation Street* (1960–). In the opening episode, Tanner examined her face in the mirror, declaring herself 'just about ready for the knacker's yard', just as Helen scrutinises her ageing face in the mirror and says, 'every wrinkle tells a dirty story'. The connection is direct: *Coronation Street* creator Tony Warren had been inspired to write his own Salford saga after seeing Delaney's play. Todd, *Tastes of Honey*, p. 130. Delaney wrote sympathetically about what she called 'the chaos of middle age' through another middle-aged female character, Kit Fresko, in her 1960 play *The Lion in Love*.

10 Sue Harper, *Women in British Cinema: Mad, Bad and Dangerous to Know* (London: Continuum, 2000), p. 112.

11 Alec Patton, 'Jazz and Music-Hall Transgressions in Theatre Workshop's Production of *A Taste of Honey*', *New Theatre Quarterly* vol. 23, no. 4 (2007), p. 336.

12 'Meeting Shelagh Delaney', *Times*, 2 February 1959, p. 12.

13 Ibid.

14 Patrick Gibbs, 'The palate and the heart', *Telegraph*, 18 September 1961, p. 9; 'Miss Tushingham is a honey!', *Middlesex County Times*, 30 September

1961, p. 19; Paul Dehn, 'A taste of brilliance', *Daily Herald*, 18 September 1961, p. 8.

15 Quoted in Patton, 'Jazz and Music-Hall Transgressions', p. 336.

16 'First draft screenplay, A Taste of Honey by Shelagh Delaney', 22 February 1960, revised 16 April 1960. Film Finances archive, box 310 (*A Taste of Honey*).

17 Lavinia Brydon, 'Shelagh Delaney (1938–2011)', in Jill Nelmes and Jule Selbo (eds), *Women Screenwriters: An International Guide* (London: Palgrave Macmillan, 2015), p. 661.

18 I have written about Tushingham's star persona in greater depth in *Female Stars of British Cinema: The Women in Question* (Edinburgh: Edinburgh University Press, 2017). This builds upon earlier work by Christine Geraghty in 'Women and 60s British Cinema: The Development of the "Darling" Girl', in Robert Murphy (ed.), *The British Cinema Book*, 3rd edn (London: BFI/Palgrave, 2009).

19 Peter Hutchings, 'Beyond the New Wave: Realism in British Cinema, 1959–63', in Murphy (ed.), *The British Cinema Book*, p. 305.

20 Shelagh Delaney, 'Never underestimate 18-year-old girls', *New York Times* (Saturday Magazine), 28 May 1961, p. 30.

21 'Shelagh Delaney on the "Angry" Young Women', *Sunday Times* (Weekly Review), 16 December 1962, p. 20.

22 Included in her collection *Sweetly Sings the Donkey* (London: Methuen, 1964).

23 Production Correspondence: Shelagh Delaney and A Taste of Honey – First Production. Joan Littlewood Archive, British Library MS 89164/5/28. Available at: <https://www.bl.uk/collection-items/letter-from-shelagh-delaney-to-joan-littlewood-sending-the-script-of-a-taste-of-honey> (accessed 8 April 2022).

24 Quoted in Todd, *Tastes of Honey*, p. 80. On Joan Littlewood's stature and significance in postwar British theatre, a good starting point is Nadine Holdsworth, *Joan Littlewood* (London: Routledge, 2006).

25 'Shelagh's first play is just Whew!', *Daily Mail*, 2 May 1958, p. 3; 'William Hickey', 'The girl who can rely on a prosperous new year', *Daily Express*, 1 January 1959, p. 3.

26 Alan Brien, 'First and last things', *The Spectator*, 5 June 1958, p. 13.

27 Ibid.

28 Robert Muller, 'The Lucretia Borgia of Salford, Lancs', *Daily Mail*, 9 February 1959, p. 6.

29 Ibid. The question of her engagement also features heavily in the television interview she did for ITN in 1959. Available at: <www.youtube.com/watch?v=SM22loR53TQ> (accessed 8 April 2022).

30 The tomboy remark is from 'Londoner's diary', *Evening Standard*, 29 December 1960, p. 6; 'William Hickey', 'Shelagh of Salford sips the sweet honey of success', *Daily Express*, 11 February 1959, p. 3.

31 Jeanette Winterson draws further telling comparisons between the treatment of Delaney and her male peers: 'Any young writer needs time and self-belief, and crucially, the belief of others, too. Orton, Osborne, Harold

Pinter were not sentimentalised and patronised – or written off – in the way that Delaney was. The reviews of *Honey* and her second play, *A Lion in Love*, read like a depressing essay in sexism. Pinter was a great writer, no doubt about it, but his early work was messy. It was Peter Hall who turned things round for him with *The Homecoming* in 1964. Nobody turned things round for Delaney.' Jeanette Winterson, 'My hero: Shelagh Delaney', *Guardian*, 18 September 2010.

32 For a detailed account of the ongoing hostilities, see John Harding, *Sweetly Sings Delaney: A Study of Shelagh Delaney's Work 1958–68* (London: Greenwich Exchange, 2014), pp. 75–84.

33 Ibid., p. 80.

34 'Shelagh's taste of money', *Daily Mail*, 2 January 1959, p. 3.

35 Ibid., and Muller, 'The Lucretia Borgia of Salford', p. 6.

36 Hoggart, *The Uses of Literacy*, p. 136.

37 'Shelagh Delaney on the "Angry" Young Women', p. 17.

38 Quoted in Littlewood, *Joan's Book*, p. 526.

39 Delaney acknowledged Littlewood's influence in her 1959 ITN interview.

40 Todd, *Tastes of Honey*, p. 135.

41 Tino Balio, *The Foreign Film Renaissance on American Screens, 1946–1973* (Madison: University of Wisconsin Press, 2010), p. 177.

42 Richardson quoted in James M. Welsh and John C. Tibbetts (eds), *The Cinema of Tony Richardson: Essays and Interviews* (New York: SUNY Press, 1999), p. 5.

43 Tony Richardson, 'The man behind an Angry Young Man', *Films and Filming*, February 1959, p. 9; Tony Richardson in 'A Free Hand', *Sight and Sound* vol. 28, no. 2 (Spring 1959), p. 64.

44 Ibid.

45 Bill Edwards, 'Production', *Kine Weekly*, 24 March 1960, p. 16.

46 John Pearson, 'The second wave', *Sunday Times* (Colour Section), 16 April 1962, p. 2.

47 Colin Young, 'Tony Richardson: An Interview in Los Angeles', *Film Quarterly* vol. 13, no. 4 (Summer 1960), p. 12.

48 Richardson, 'The man behind an Angry Young Man', p. 9.

49 Young, 'Tony Richardson: An Interview in Los Angeles', p. 12.

50 'The kitchen bath school', *Daily Mail*, 15 April 1961, p. 3.

51 Tony Richardson, 'The two worlds of the cinema', *Films and Filming*, June 1961, p. 7.

52 Tony Richardson, *Long Distance Runner: A Memoir* (London: Faber, 1993), p. 142.

53 Quoted in Alexander Walker, *Hollywood England: The British Film Industry in the Sixties* (London: Michael Joseph, 1974), p. 91.

54 Sarah Street, 'Film Finances and the British New Wave', *Historical Journal of Film, Radio and Television* vol. 34, no. 1 (March 2014), p. 24.

55 Letter from John Croydon to Robert Garrett, 30 May 1960. Film Finances archive, box 310 (*A Taste of Honey*).

56 Ibid.

57 Ibid.

58 Countersigned agreement between Woodfall Film Productions Ltd and Shelagh Delaney, 29 February 1960, and 'First draft screenplay'.

59 Letter from Croydon to Garrett, 7 February 1961. Film Finances archive, box 310 (*A Taste of Honey*).

60 Littlewood, *Joan's Book*, p. 515. Interestingly, Littlewood also cites critic Alan Brien suggesting the play was 'written as if it were a film script' (p. 519).

61 Richardson, 'The two worlds of the cinema', p. 41.

62 Letter from Croydon to Garrett, 30 May 1960.

63 Reisz quoted in Welsh and Tibbetts (eds), *The Cinema of Tony Richardson*, p. 27.

64 For more on Brinton's place within traditions of British production design, see Laurie Ede, *British Film Design: A History* (London: I. B. Tauris, 2010), and specifically on the 1960s, Richard Farmer, Laura Mayne, Duncan Petrie and Melanie Williams, *Transformation and Tradition in 1960s British Cinema* (Edinburgh: Edinburgh University Press, 2019).

65 Ralph Brinton, 'The New Realism in British Films', *Journal of the Society of Film and Television Arts* no. 11 (Spring 1963), p. 9.

66 Richardson also had a hand in costuming characters: Dora Bryan recalled how, during a shopping trip with him, he wanted the tightest possible fitting clothes for Helen, who he felt would want to show off her figure. Costumes were also sourced more informally, with Jo's baggy jumper actually belonging to Rita Tushingham's brother. DVD commentary for 2002 BFI release of *A Taste of Honey*.

67 Walter Lassally, *Itinerant Cameraman* (London: John Murray, 1987), p. 64.

68 Ibid., p. 69.

69 Correspondence quoted in Aldgate, *Censorship and the Permissive Society*, p. 138.

70 Richardson, 'The two worlds of the cinema', p. 41. Being able to pay them less may also have figured in this. Rita Tushingham only drew £500 for her work on the film, compared to the higher salaries of more experienced artistes like Bryan.

71 Peter Evans, 'John Osborne seeking ugly girl for Taste of Honey', *Daily Express*, 2 March 1960, p. 4.

72 Dench said she was 'just pipped' to the role. Quoted in Williams, *Female Stars of British Cinema*, p. 173.

73 Richardson, *Long Distance Runner*, p. 121.

74 Ibid.

75 Peter Evans, 'Found: the ugly girl', *Daily Express*, 27 April 1960, p. 12; Ernest Betts, 'Ugly mug!', *People*, 17 September 1961. Osborne quoted in *Daily Express* article.

76 Marje Proops, 'Honey for the bread and butter girl', *Daily Mirror*, 13 September 1961, p. 11.

77 *A Taste of Honey* pressbook, BFI Reuben Library.

78 Ad featured in *Kine Weekly*, 14 September 1961.

79 Richardson, *Long Distance Runner*, p. 121. Critics Alexander Walker and Dilys Powell described him variously as looking like a Plantagenet and a Borzoi. Melvin became the 'keeper of the flame' of the original production in the process of its translation to screen, later taking on the mantle of archivist for Theatre Workshop. See Michael Billington,

'O what a lovely archive', *Guardian*, 1 February 2021.

80 Danquah was the son of a high-ranking Ghanaian politician and also at the heart of London's gay artistic circles, at one point sharing his home with the artist Francis Bacon as well as Danquah's partner Peter Pollock. The Billy Dee Williams suggestion comes from the crossplot dated 25 May 1960. Film Finances archive, box 310 (*A Taste of Honey*).

81 Richardson, 'The two worlds of the cinema', p. 41.

82 2002 DVD commentary. The film's pressbook suggests the casting was 'a shock. Traditional minds boggled when Dora Bryan, the Queen of English parlour comedies, was chosen to play Helen.'

83 Crossplot, 25 May 1960.

84 Robert Murphy, 'New Morning: Optimism and Resilience in Tony Richardson's *A Taste of Honey* and *The Loneliness of the Long Distance Runner*', *Journal of British Cinema and Television* vol. 11, no. 3 (2014), p. 385.

85 Daily production progress reports. Film Finances archive, box 310 (*A Taste of Honey*).

86 Richardson, *Long Distance Runner*, p. 121.

87 Richardson in Gordon Gow, 'Within the cocoon', *Films and Filming*, June 1977, p. 14.

88 David Nathan, 'The dingy, drab doorway to fame', *Daily Herald*, 8 April 1961.

89 Daily production progress reports.

90 Julian Holland, *Evening News*, 15 May 1961.

91 'First draft screenplay', p. 1.

92 Compare it to Tony Richardson's own non-compliance with school PE: 'They could put me on a football field, but they couldn't make me kick a ball. They could make me change into a singlet and shorts, but I wouldn't go through their exercises with any will or effort.' Richardson, *Long Distance Runner*, p. 52. This idea of sporting refusal would reach its apotheosis in his next film, *The Loneliness of the Long Distance Runner*.

93 Robert Shail, *Tony Richardson* (Manchester: Manchester University Press, 2012), p. 31.

94 Hoggart, *The Uses of Literacy*, pp. 193, 132.

95 The trick of making the statues look more mobile was self-borrowed by Walter Lassally from the Free Cinema documentary *We Are the Lambeth Boys* (1959).

96 Or it could be in anticipation of the slogan outside a blackened Victorian church, 'God washes whitest of all', the clergy striving for contemporary relevance in a commercialised world.

97 Terry Lovell, 'Landscapes and Stories in 1960s British Realism', *Screen* vol. 31, no. 4 (Winter 1990), p. 368. Lovell draws extensively on Carolyn Steedman's coruscating work of auto-ethnography, *Landscape for a Good Woman* (London: Virago, 1986), to make sense of how *A Taste of Honey* also presents working-class female lives 'lived out on the borderlands, lives for which the central interpretive devices of the culture don't quite work' (p. 5).

98 Dehn, 'A taste of brilliance', p. 8.

99 Lovell, 'Landscapes and Stories', p. 376.

100 This tactic was discussed in Justine King, 'Crossing Thresholds: The Contemporary British Woman's Film', in Andrew Higson (ed.), *Dissolving Views: Key Writings on British Cinema* (London: Cassell, 1996), p. 219, and expanded in the introduction to Melanie Bell and Melanie Williams (eds), *British Women's Cinema* (London: Routledge, 2009).

101 It has a literary parallel in Celia Brayfield's recent overview of women writers of the 1960s, which productively places Delaney at the head of a cohort of feminist writers including Edna O'Brien, Lynne Reid-Banks and Nell Dunn rather than the usual male company of Osborne, Sillitoe, Wesker et al. Celia Brayfield, *Rebel Writers: The Accidental Feminists* (London: Bloomsbury, 2019).

102 See Simon Frith and Howard Horne's *Art into Pop* (London: Routledge, 2016) and Mike Roberts, *How Art Made Pop – And Pop Became Art* (London: Tate Publishing, 2018), for useful overviews of this phenomenon.

103 In an earlier draft the poem was Charles Woolf's 'The Burial of Sir John Moore after Corunna' but this was changed to have Jo dreamily enraptured over Ruth's exile and consolation in birdsong. Final screenplay dated 3 March 1961, p. 15. Film Finances archive, box 310 (*A Taste of Honey*).

104 'Shelagh Delaney's Salford', *Monitor* (BBC). Dir. Ken Russell, tx 15 September 1960.

105 'First draft screenplay', p. 20.

106 Ibid., p. 21.

107 Ibid.

108 'Shelagh Delaney on the "Angry" Young Women', p. 17.

109 Ibid.

110 Shail, *Tony Richardson*, p. 33.

111 MacColl was a founder member of Theatre Workshop and Joan Littlewood's first husband.

112 *A Taste of Honey* pressbook, BFI Reuben Library.

113 'Editorial: The British Cinema', p. 5; Thomas Elsaesser, 'Between Style and Ideology', *Monogram* no. 3 (1972), p. 5.

114 Andrew Higson, 'Space, Place, Spectacle: Landscape and Townscape in the "Kitchen Sink" Film', in Higson (ed.), *Dissolving Views*, p. 149. Based on an article first published in 1984.

115 John Hill, *Sex, Class and Realism: British Cinema 1956–1963* (London: BFI, 1986), pp. 129, 131.

116 Higson, 'Space, Place, Spectacle', pp. 150–2.

117 Ibid.

118 Hutchings, 'Beyond the New Wave', p. 309; B. F. Taylor, *The British New Wave: A Certain Tendency?* (Manchester: Manchester University Press, 2006), p. 119.

119 Ibid., p. 111. Hutchings and Murphy have also historicised Higson's and Hill's responses to the New Wave in relation to suspicions of humanist realism dominating screen theory in the 1980s, constructing 'the open-minded liberalism of Richardson, Reisz and Anderson as inadequate and deficient' (Murphy, 'New Morning', p. 393), leading to an 'almost palpable sense of disappointment that the films concerned do not go far enough' in their attempt to present working-class subjectivity, representing instead a 'failed revolution' (Hutchings, 'Beyond the New Wave', p. 309).

120 Hill, *Sex, Class and Realism*, p. 131.

121 Taylor, *The British New Wave*, p. 58.

122 'First draft screenplay', p. 15.

123 Higson, 'Space, Place, Spectacle', p. 151. The Salford artist L. S. Lowry is obviously a highly relevant figure in relation to this, as someone who often painted working-class locales and communities from an elevated position and whose own class positioning was ambivalent, and his paintings adorned all Salford schoolrooms (gifted by the city corporation), including those where Delaney was taught. But there is insufficient space to explore this here.

124 Ibid., p. 153.

125 Ibid., p. 148.

126 Ibid., p. 154.

127 Ibid.

128 Andrew Klevan, *Disclosure of the Everyday: Undramatic Achievement in Narrative Film* (Trowbridge: Flicks Books, 2000).

129 David Forrest, 'Shane Meadows and the British New Wave: Britain's Hidden Art Cinema', *Studies in European Cinema* vol. 6, no. 2 (2009), p. 195.

130 Ibid., p. 201.

131 It's worth noting too the scant attention paid to audience response to the imagery presented. Although Terry Lovell suggests that the rooftop vantage point of *Coronation Street*'s opening titles 'opens up a broad chasm between the observing eye of the camera and that of the observer within the landscape' (Lovell, 'Landscapes and Stories', p. 369), how does that equate to its status as popular drama watched by millions, many of them we might reasonably surmise within the same social classes depicted on screen? Singer Cilla Black's response to the first episode, showing a character mending a bicycle puncture in the living room just as her dad was doing exactly the same, was to think, 'Wow, they're as common as us' (quoted in Kynaston, *Modernity Britain*, p. 485). The programme's popularity seemed to hinge more on recognition and identification rather than any voyeuristic 'broad chasm'. This territory of localised reception among the communities being represented is explored in Jonny Smith, 'Whatever people say I am, that's what I'm not: A Reception Study of 1960s British Social Realism', MA dissertation (University of Manchester, 2017).

132 Shelagh Delaney, *A Taste of Honey* (London: Methuen, 1959), p. 86.

133 Stuart Maconie, *Pies and Prejudice: In Search of the North* (London: Ebury, 2008), p. 268.

134 Lovell, 'Landscapes and Stories', p. 370.

135 Brydon, 'Shelagh Delaney', pp. 655–6.

136 'First draft screenplay', pp. 3–4.

137 Todd, *Tastes of Honey*, p. 71; Brydon, 'Shelagh Delaney', p. 655.

138 Lovell, 'Landscapes and Stories', pp. 372–3.

139 Todd, *Tastes of Honey*, p. 145.

140 'First draft screenplay', p. 31. Delaney juxtaposes different funfairs in the film in Hoggartian fashion, writing that the Whit Week fair 'is meant as a deliberate contrast to the earlier sequence in Blackpool. The fairground itself is small and toy-like. The roundabouts and sideshows are all painted in old-fashioned ways, and very stylized. JO and GEOFFREY's enjoyment has a quaintness and innocence about it in marked contrast to Helen and Peter's earlier carry on' (p. 50).

141 'First draft screenplay', p. 55.

142 'Editorial: The British Cinema', p. 5.

143 Delaney, *A Taste of Honey*, p. 85.

144 Iona and Peter Opie, *The Lore and Language of Schoolchildren* (Oxford: Oxford University Press, 1959). Some of the rhymes that appear in their book, such as 'I say, what a smasher', also appear in the film (the follow-up line, 'Look at her she's getting fatter', alludes to Jo's pregnancy before she even knows about it, making the children a kind of all-knowing Greek Chorus).

145 Quoted in Kynaston, *Modernity Britain*, p. 706. One of the kids grew up into New Labour politician Hazel Blears.

146 This double perspective also derived from being sent away to Lytham St Annes in childhood for an extended convalescence from a bone infection, a formative experience she returned to in later writing.

147 Kynaston, *Modernity Britain*, p. 12. Kynaston cross-refers to Young and Wilmott's influential 1957 study *Family and Kinship in East London* that found similar things going on in the resettlement of Bethnal Green residents in new estates in Essex.

148 Ibid., p. 289. Delaney's comments are from the *Monitor* documentary. Her involvement in plans to convert the old Salford Hippodrome theatre into an arts centre seems to have been a factor in the plans stalling and the fine building being demolished instead. Recounted in Harding, *Sweetly Sings Delaney*, pp. 106–13.

149 Shelagh Delaney, 'A taste of money', *Daily Mail*, 22 February 1992, pp. 22–3. They also asked Kingsley Amis, Alan Sillitoe, Keith Waterhouse, Stan Barstow and Margaret Drabble to imagine what happened next to their iconic protagonists Jim Dixon, Colin Smith, Billy Fisher, Vic Brown and Rosamund Stacey.

150 Ibid.

151 Ibid.

152 Ibid.

153 Brydon, 'Shelagh Delaney', p. 661.

154 Todd, *Tastes of Honey*, p. 130. She wasn't interested in developing other work for Granada either but did agree to provide scripts for the BBC series *Z Cars*.

155 Andy Medhurst, '*Victim*: Text as Context', in Higson (ed.), *Dissolving Views*, pp. 117–32.

156 The 'proto-mod' comment is in Robert Murphy, *Sixties British Cinema* (London: BFI, 1992), p. 50. For more on Vince clothes as queer discourse, see Justin Bengry, 'Peacock Revolution: Mainstreaming Queer Styles in Post-War Britain, 1945–1967', *Socialist History* no. 36 (2010), pp. 55–68.

157 Robin Griffiths, 'Sad and Angry: Queers in 1960s British Cinema', in Griffiths (ed.), *British Queer Cinema* (London: Routledge, 2006), p. 79.

158 2011 Q&A with Rita Tushingham, Murray Melvin and Walter Lassally at BFI Southbank, included on the 2018 BFI Blu-ray release of *A Taste of Honey*.

159 William L. Horne, 'Greatest Pleasures', in Welsh and Tibbetts (eds), *The Cinema of Tony Richardson*, p. 121. Robert Shail also suggests Richardson's 'favourite thematic concern' was 'siding with outcasts, rebels and those marginalised by society'. Shail, *Tony Richardson*, p. 33. Although Robert Murphy points out that Danquah and Melvin – 'both of them gay – contrast sharply with the aggressively heterosexual protagonists' of other New Wave films (Murphy, 'New Morning', p. 385), Robin Griffiths makes the interesting counter-observation about how thoroughly imbricated with gay creativity the whole of the British New Wave was, but notably leading directors Lindsay Anderson and John Schlesinger (Griffiths, 'Sad and Angry: Queers in 1960s British Cinema', p. 79).

160 Richard Dyer, 'Coming Out as Going In: The Homosexual as a Sad Young Man', in *The Culture of Queers* (London: Routledge, 2002). Dyer identifies Geoff as a prime example of the type but mentions his own personal identification with him as a teenager: 'I thought I virtually was Geoff in *A Taste of Honey*' (p. 116).

161 DVD commentary for 2002 BFI release of *A Taste of Honey*.

162 'First draft screenplay', p. 54.

163 Todd, *Tastes of Honey*, p. 145.

164 Ibid. The badge reflects Delaney's own allegiance.

165 There are worrying aspects of this possible conflation of Irishness and non-whiteness with the darker understanding of 'daftness' as mental defection. The child that Jo refers to is played by a boy who appears to have Downs Syndrome, imbuing her comments on maternal irresponsibility ('the harm she does having children') with ableist eugenicist undertones beyond concerns about cleanliness and poverty. I have been unable to ascertain any information about the boy or his casting from the production documentation I have been able to access.

166 Lovell, 'Landscapes and Stories', p. 374.

167 'First draft screenplay', p. 77.

168 Ibid., p. 81. She also called Geoff a 'pansified little freak' (p. 82), which the BBFC took issue with, less out of gay solidarity than fearfulness around inflammatory language.

169 A planned follow-up was going to culminate with the protagonist being eaten by cannibals before Albert Finney suggested that this wouldn't curry favour with the money men: 'We'd never have got the backing for it. Heroes like Steve McQueen don't get eaten.' Philip Oakes, 'Finney sings a song of life', *Sunday Times*, 28 August 1977, p. 31.

170 Lovell, 'Landscapes and Stories', p. 372.

171 Hall's review in *Universities and Left Review*, quoted in Harding, *Sweetly Sings Delaney*, p. 64.

172 'First draft screenplay', p. 85.

173 Ibid., p. 84.

174 Hill, *Sex, Class and Realism*, p. 106; Murphy, 'New Morning', p. 395.

175 'Film virtues in *A Taste of Honey*', *Times*, 13 September 1961, p. 14.

176 To which both Labour leader Hugh Gaitskill and soon-to-be-infamous War

Minister John Profumo were invited, though it is not clear if either attended. 'Film invitation to Mr Gaitskill', *Sunday Telegraph*, 3 September 1961, p. 16.

177 Thomas Wiseman, 'Films', *Sunday Express*, 17 September 1961; Donald Zec, 'The odd girls out', *Daily Mirror*, 25 October 1961, p. 15; William Whitebait, 'Films', *New Statesman*, 15 September 1961.

178 Frank Hazell, 'Showmanship', *Kine Weekly*, 18 January 1962, p. 24.

179 Dehn, 'A taste of brilliance', p. 8; Isabel Quigly, 'Vagrants', *Spectator*, 22 September 1961. One surprising fan was novelist E. M. Forster, who thought *A Taste of Honey* 'gained a lot in its film version from the wonderful use they made of those moors and streets'. J. W. Lambert, 'Mr Forster at the play', *Sunday Times*, 4 August 1963, p. 20.

180 Leonard Mosley, 'How do you like a girl to look?', *Daily Express*, 15 September 1961, p. 4.

181 Penelope Gilliatt, 'Woodfall strikes again', *Observer*, 17 September 1961, p. 27.

182 Peter Simple, 'Way of the world', *Daily Telegraph*, 5 January 1962, p. 12.

183 Duncan Petrie, 'Bryanston Films: An Experiment in Cooperative Independent Film Production and Distribution', *Historical Journal of Film, Radio and Television* vol. 38, no. 1 (2018), p. 103.

184 Josh Billings, 'Family fare triumphs at box-office', *Kine Weekly*, 14 December 1961, p. 9.

185 <https://m.imdb.com/event/ev0000464/1962/1?ref_=m_ttawd_ev_7> (accessed 8 April 2022).

186 Truffaut in a personal letter of April 1963, quoted in Horne, 'Greatest Pleasures', p. 88.

187 DVD commentary for 2002 BFI release of *A Taste of Honey*.

188 Ian Pye, 'Some mothers do 'ave 'em', *NME*, 7 June 1986. For a thorough account of The Smiths and Morrissey's imbrication with the British New Wave, see Cecilia Mello, 'I Don't Owe You Anything: The Smiths and Kitchen-Sink Cinema', in Sean Campbell and Colin Coulter (eds), *Why Pamper Life's Complexities? Essays on The Smiths* (Manchester: Manchester University Press, 2010), pp. 135–55. Also relevant is L. K. Wallace, 'This One Is Different Because It's Ours: The Ordinary, The Extraordinary, and The Working-Class Artist in A Taste of Honey', *Journal of Popular Culture* vol. 50, no. 4 (2017), pp. 778–95.

189 Tim Jonze, 'Bigmouth strikes again and again: why Morrissey fans feel so betrayed', *Guardian*, 30 May 2019.

190 Owen Hatherley, *The Ministry of Nostalgia* (London: Verso, 2016), p. 194; Sarah Manavis, 'History-themed Facebook groups have become a magnet for racist content', *New Statesman*, 17 June 2019. Available at: <https://www.newstatesman.com/science-tech/2019/06/history-themed-facebook-groups-have-become-a-magnet-for-racist-content> (accessed 8 April 2022).

191 Simon Heffer, 'Talking Pictures became the soothing, nostalgic delight Britain needed during lockdown', *Daily Telegraph*, 25 July 2020.

192 As Julian Petley and Andrew Roberts suggest, not only is Heffer using the channel to mount 'an overt attack on aspects of the present which Heffer despises', but his understanding of their output, which frequently offers a darker, bleaker vision of the past, is skewed. 'Culture Wars, Talking Pictures and the Telegraph: Part One', *EUP Blog*, 23 September 2020. Available at: <https://euppublishingblog. com/2020/09/23/culture-wars-one/> (accessed 8 April 2022).

193 The film's multiculturalism is not only enacted through Jimmy but through what its 'candid camera' technique reveals about Britain at the time, such as the young Asian men among those walking the Blackpool promenade. This is akin to Lynda Nead's deployment of Laura Mulvey's technique of slowing or freezing film to bring out visually fleeting details, revealing the significant presence of people of colour visiting the 1951 Festival of Britain. Lynda Nead, *The Tiger in the Smoke: Art and Culture in Post-War Britain* (New Haven, CT: Yale University Press, 2017), pp. 211–13.

Credits

A Taste of Honey
UK
1961

Directed by
Tony Richardson
Production Supervisor
Leigh Aman
Assistant Producer
Michael Holden
Producer
Tony Richardson
Assistant Director
Peter Yates
Screenplay by
Shelagh Delaney and
Tony Richardson
Based on the play by
Shelagh Delaney

© Woodfall Films 1961
Bryanston
British Lion

Director of Photography
Walter Lassally
Camera Operator
Desmond Davis
Editor
Antony Gibbs
Art Director
Ralph Brinton
Assistant Art Director
Ted Marshall
Wardrobe
Sophie Devine
Barbara Gillett

Unit Manager
Roy Millichip
Continuity
Rita Davison
Music
John Addison, performed
by Virtuoso Ensemble
Sound Editors
Don Challis
Roy Hyde
Sound Recordist
Charles Poulton

CAST
Rita Tushingham
Jo
Dora Bryan
Helen
Murray Melvin
Geoffrey
Paul Danquah
Jimmy
Robert Stephens
Peter
David Boliver
Bert
Moira Kaye
Doris
Herbert Smith
shoe shop proprietor
Valerie Scarden
customer
Rosalie Scace
nurse
Eunice Black
school mistress

Production Details
35mm
1.75:1
Black and white
Running time:
100 minutes

Release Details
UK theatrical release
on 1 October 1961 by
Bryanston Films/British
Lion Film Corporation
US theatrical release
on 30 April 1962 by
Continental Distributing